Designing for the User with OVID:

Bridging User Interface

Design and Software

Engineering

Dave Roberts
Dick Berry
Scott Isensee
John Mullaly

MACMILLAN
TECHNICAL
PUBLISHING
U·S·A

Macmillan Technical Publishing
201 West 103rd Street
Indianapolis, IN 46290 USA

International Standard Book Number: 1-57870-101-5

Library of Congress Catalog Card Number: 98-85558

2001   00   99   98   4   3   2   1

Interpretation of the printing code: The rightmost double-digit number is the year of the book's printing; the rightmost single-digit, the number of the book's printing. For example, the printing code 98-1 shows that the first printing of the book occurred in 1998.

Composed in Bergamo by Macmillan Computer Publishing

Printed in the United States of America

Trademark Acknowledgments

Warning and Disclaimer

Permissions

Vice President
Don Fowley

Associate Publisher
Jim LeValley

Executive Editor
Ann Trump Daniel

Managing Editor
Caroline Roop

Development Editor
Kitty Wilson Jarrett

Project Editor
Jennifer Chisholm

Indexer
Tim Wright

Acquisitions Coordinator
Amy Lewis

Book Designer
Gary Adair

Cover Designer
Karen Ruggles

Production Team Supervisor
Daniela Raderstorf

Production
Megan Wade

Feedback Information

At Macmillan Technical Publishing, our goal is to create in-depth technical books of the highest quality and value. Each book is crafted with care and precision, undergoing rigorous development that involves the unique expertise of members from the professional technical community.

Readers' feedback is a natural continuation of this process. If you have any comments regarding how we could improve the quality of this book, or otherwise alter it to better suit your needs, you can contact us at softwareengineering@mcp.com. Please make sure to include the book title and ISBN in your message.

We greatly appreciate your assistance.

About the Authors

Dave Roberts is a senior software designer working in IBM's Ease of Use Strategy and Design group in Warwick, United Kingdom. Dave has been with IBM since 1974. He has worked in many areas of computer development and support, including hardware design, systems support, and the design of OS/2 Presentation Manager. Since 1986 he has worked on user-interface architecture topics, including all versions of Common User Access (CUA). He was a principal architect of the 1992 version of CUA.

Dick Berry is a senior technical staff member in the Ease of Use Architecture and Design Group at IBM's Austin, Texas, development lab. He was the lead architect for three generations of IBM's Common User Access, a user interface style widely used by Windows and OS/2 applications. Berry holds 18 patents in user interface design and is an elected member of the IBM Academy of Technology and a member of ACM SIGCHI.

Scott Isensee is a user-interface architect with IBM in Austin, Texas, where he works on advanced user-interface design architecture, guidelines, and methodologies. He was user-interface team leader for development of the Common Desktop Environment (CDE), a graphical user interface for UNIX. Scott is a member of the ANSI and ISO committees writing software user-interface and usability standards. He has numerous patents and publications on topics related to user-interface design. He holds master's degrees in computer science and industrial psychology. He is a certified professional ergonomist (CPE). Scott is an author of the recent book *The Art of Rapid Prototyping*.

John Mullaly is a user-interface architect and designer with IBM's advanced human–computer interaction group in Austin, Texas. He joined IBM in 1987 as a computer graphics specialist and has been working in the field of HCI since 1992. He holds a bachelor of science degree from the New York Institute of Technology, where he studied math, art, and computer science. John is a professional member of the Society of Design and Process Science (SDPS) and the Industrial Designer's Society of America (IDSA).

Contents at a Glance

Table of Contents

Foreword

User interface designers face a big challenge. On one hand are the implementors, the programmers struggling to churn out enough content to make steadily doubling tele-computing capacity pay off for its users. On the other hand are the users, Apple's "rest of us," those who determine worth through buying the software that pays everybody else's salaries.

Getting these groups to work together is no job for quick fixes. But this book doesn't promise that—just a novel way to facilitate interaction and collaboration between programmers and users. This is a refreshing alternative to the pervasive assumption that users and implementors will inevitably misunderstand one another. I plan to incorporate this approach in my own work and hope you will see the worth of this in your work also.

I would rather not admit how long it took for me to appreciate that differences between individuals are not small. Even in culturally homogeneous circles, and even when we speak the same language and were educated in similar schools, the ways people view the world and express their identities within it can be very different. The results of today's communication struggles can be devastating to the quality of techni-cal creations such as software.

For example, consider UNIX's command-line user interface. Kernighan's *Software Tools*, to pick one book among many, describes a philosophy that implementors such as I continue to find deeply compelling—that software tools should be small, handle very narrow jobs, and be combined with other tools to solve the problem at hand. As a result, the early UNIX tool *mail* did not paginate on the grounds that this should be handled by a separate tool. When users complained that their mail scrolled by too quickly to read, it was the user's fault for not understanding the small tools philoso-phy. It took years to recognize this problem as a miscommunication between people with very different views of the world, not as the fault of either side.

By contrast, consider the philosophy behind IBM's RealPhone application, which is discussed in this book. The core value is that software should be consistent with how the users view their world without sending them to the manual to learn how they "ought" to think about their work.

The point is not that the implementor's worldview is wrongminded and extinct—quite the opposite. Today's user-friendly applications are indisputably produced by implementors who have perfectly sound reasons for seeing the world differently from other people. After all, the implementors' job requires that we see the computer from the other side of the screen. Although users have sound reasons for concentrating on surface appearance—how things appear on the screen—we have equally valid reasons for concentrating on underlying form—how it all works inside.

Designing for the User with OVID: Bridging User Interface Design and Software Engineering assumes from the outset that diversity is the solution, not the problem. It then moves on to provide techniques for bridging the chasm in worldview and vocabulary that would otherwise keep users and implementors from cooperating due to lack of understanding. Reduced to bare essentials, the user-interface designer's task is to translate the user's view of the solution into problem statements implementors can understand.

It's not easy to get people with different worldviews, skills, norms, and terminology to work together. But this is exactly what must be done to build software that doesn't disappoint. The user interface designer just stands in the middle, translating signals from each side into meanings the other is able to understand. It's really just as simple as that—and as difficult.

The belief that people with diverse worldviews, priorities, and languages can leverage their diversity as a strength ultimately drew me from software engineering to my current work in organizational learning. This belief resulted from a growing conviction that users actually do know what they need. Their understanding, however, is in terms of surface appearance, a "hip" artistic way of understanding that isn't accessible to engineers trained to a "square" scientific focus on underlying form.

This gap between users and engineers is an often-noticed but seldom-recognized issue. In this book, the authors not only recognize the impact of the issue; they go further, addressing the issue through the use of OVID. The gap is not likely to close on its own, so this book is of critical importance in our endeavors to leverage differing worldviews in order to successfully develop software in combination with users, user interface designers, and programmers.

Brad Cox
June 21, 1997

Dr. Brad Cox is a faculty member in the George Mason University Program on Social and Organizational Learning. He authored *Object-Oriented Programming: An Evolutionary Approach*, which is generally credited with launching today's industrywide enthusiasm for object technology. He is the cofounder of the Stepstone Corporation.

Preface

The concepts and approaches described in this book have evolved through our experiences with user-interface design dating back almost two decades. In 1978 one of the authors developed a notation for describing menus and entry fields displayed on a screen and user interactions with those interface elements. The motivation for this work was to convey a complete and unambiguous specification of the user interface to the implementors. The implementation was an office system intended for use by secretaries and administrative personnel, so simplicity and ease-of-use were major factors.

Throughout the late 1970s and early 1980s, there were many efforts to achieve ease-of-use through standardizing interface elements. The common thread in most of these approaches was consistency. Lacking an in-depth understanding of the factors affecting usability, most teams faced with developing an approach to usability simply implemented standards. Principles of interface design were not widely known or understood and only began to be appreciated when developers from Xerox PARC, and later Apple, published papers documenting the evolution of the Star, Lisa, and Macintosh. These efforts began to capture the imaginations of a new genre of designer—one that was convinced there were principles and methodologies for user interface design that could be applied to achieve much more usable products.

The impetus for the major advancements in which the authors participated came somewhat later, in early 1988, when a group within IBM began to explore the concepts underlying an object-oriented user interface (OOUI). Tony Temple, now an IBM Fellow, brought together a small team of top designers from across IBM, with ongoing participation by Tandy Trower from Microsoft. Dick Berry, the lead architect of IBM's Common User Access (CUA); Dave Roberts, a key designer of the OS/2 Presentation Manager; and Tony Temple were the principal architects, with frequent reviews, consultations, and suggestions from system and application development groups across IBM and Microsoft. Tandy Trower is currently the director of advanced user interface design at Microsoft. Cliff Reeves, currently the senior product manager for Notes/Domino at Lotus Development Corporation, was a key organizer and supporter of the team.

Over the next two years, this team analyzed, experimented with, and mapped out the fundamental concepts and relationships that are the basis of an OOUI. Many of these concepts were embodied in the CUA interface style, which was widely adopted by IBM and Microsoft applications beginning in 1989.

Ultimately, Cliff Reeves formed a group that created and published the next generation of CUA (IBM 1992) and implemented a functional prototype of the Workplace User Model, as it came to be called. The prototype was developed using Smalltalk, with assistance from Knowledge Systems Corporation in Cary, North Carolina. The implementation effort alone took approximately seven person-years. Several major user studies were conducted using this prototype. These studies provided valuable information, leading all team members to fully endorse iterative development using prototypes. Major elements of the object-oriented interface style are visible today in IBM OS/2 Warp's Workplace Shell and Microsoft's Windows 95 and NT.

Our first endeavor at formalizing and documenting an OOUI design approach was published in the *CUA Style Guide*, first printed by IBM in 1991 and subsequently by Que Corporation in 1992 (IBM 1992). Many of the fundamental concepts are carried through and strengthened in today's version. The importance of the user's conceptual model and the designer's model (Figure P.1) remains as a central theme. These factors, along with what we felt was an overemphasis on "look and feel" at the time, caused us to publish the "iceberg" analogy of usability in the 1991 version of CUA. This analogy, which stresses the importance of conceptual information carried in a system's object model, is still used frequently in current texts. It is described in full in Chapter 2.

The disciplines of object-oriented analysis (OOA) and object-oriented design (OOD) have come to the forefront in support of object-oriented programming in the 1990s. Along with these new analysis and design approaches, new tools to aid program designers have been developed. During our use of some of these tools in the development of software components in early 1995, we recognized a significant opportunity for applying them to the task of user interface design.

Recently we have been exploring a new style of user interface: one based on making the presentation and behavior of objects closely resemble objects that users are familiar with from their real-world experiences. Scott Isensee and John Mullaly joined the collaboration during the design of the IBM RealPhone, which is an experiment in applying principles of real-world object look and feel to a computer-based speakerphone. We first used the design tool Rational Rose during the design of the RealPhone. During this experience we identified deficiencies in state diagrams that led Dave Roberts to develop a program that generates state tables from Rose state diagrams.

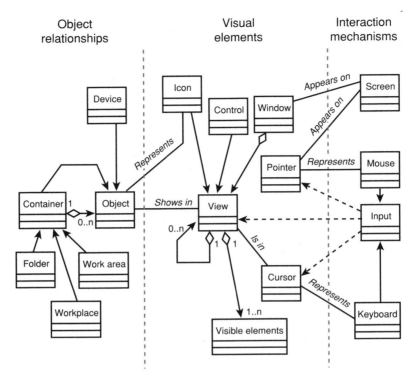

FIGURE P.1 *The CUA designer's model.*

Note

Many good software modeling tools are available. We mention Rational Rose (a product of Rational Software, www.rational.com) only because it is the one we have the most experience with.

The Object, View, and Interaction Design (OVID) methodology is a result of further refinement of several aspects evident in our prior work, with the addition of notations and formalisms made easily available by tools. We expect OVID to be an evolving methodology. Already we have recognized opportunities for additional specifications (for example, to help convey abstract aspects of object views to graphic designers).

We have also identified deficiencies in the set of tools currently available. But let us not be too critical. They were not designed specifically for the task of user interface design. We are beginning to develop a list of enhancements for the methodology and for the tools. Perhaps one day in the near future we might see OOA/OOD tools with full support for OOUI design built in. Imagine a tool that started with the output of task analysis, helped you identify the objects that users need to do their tasks, prompted you through decomposition of the tasks into views with state diagrams that ensured every user situation was covered, and ultimately generated a specification for each view to which graphics designers could apply their artistic skills, achieving various styles to please and satisfy a variety of discerning users. And, by the way, it would also generate the classes for the code. What could be more conducive to the highly productive, rapid prototyping, iterative design environment that all designers envision?

Dedication

We dedicate this book to our families, who supported us through yet another demand on our time: Carol, Stephen, Suzanne, Annette, and Madison Berry; Gillian Roberts; Dawn Isensee; and Kazumi T. Mullaly.

Acknowledgments

This journey began almost a decade ago, with our first explorations into object-oriented user interfaces. Obviously, scores of people have contributed to the concepts and features that we see in today's systems and applications. Mentioning everyone would be impossible, but a few individuals remain ever present in our minds, for they were the ones there at the birth of the concepts or they were the ones who nurtured the ideas to maturity and made them real. They believed in the paradigm shift and made it happen.

To Tony Temple, for providing the initial spark and continuing to provide the leadership and vision for nearly a decade; to Cliff Reeves, for believing in the new direction enough to move to Cary, North Carolina, and recruit an outstanding team to develop and deliver the first version; to Tandy Trower at Microsoft, for keeping our feet on the ground and maintaining a focus on practical application development issues; to Steve Fleming, Pat Keane, and Lee Griffin, for creative ideas and criticisms in the early days; to David Schwartz, Joe Coulombe, Sue Henshaw, Chuck Schafer, Cindy Roosken, and Theo Mandel, for devoting several years of their careers to developing, testing, and teaching the new paradigm and very early versions of the methodology; to Rod Smith, for providing the invaluable application developer's perspective; to Lee Reiswig and the OS/2 shell development team, Lori Brown, Peter Magid, and James Taylor, who early on recognized the potential of the Workplace Model and delivered the first systems implementation in the form of the OS/2 Workplace Shell; to Didier Bardon and Shirley Martin, who continue to work with us in applying and evolving the approach; to Scott Morgan and Craig Swearingen, who have provided programming support as we have developed interfaces using OVID; to Paul Waldo, who provided management support throughout the project; to Dan Best, who helped produce figures; to Ann Trump Daniel and Kitty Jarrett, who guided the book through the publishing process; and finally, to those who volunteered to be the first to try our tutorials: Alan Tannenbaum, Vanessa Donnelley, Andy Smith, Mark Evans, Richard Hodgkinson, John Cook, Todd Wiese, and others too numerous to list.

Introduction

Despite the promise and often exaggerated claims of improved ease-of-use, many believe that today's personal computers are rapidly becoming more complex, suffering from a functional bloat, which is actually making them more difficult to use, raising barriers to potential new users. At the same time, computer education is becoming more pervasive. Classes on keyboarding and computer literacy are becoming commonplace in primary and secondary schools. But despite the ever-increasing literacy of the general public, there still exists a very large number of potential personal computer (PC) users who remain skeptical and even fear interacting with a computer. By some analysts' reports, sales of personal computers are beginning to flatten, while nearly 50% of the U.S. population remains an untapped marketplace. There is potential for improved user interfaces to significantly expand the computer market.

Today's systems provide more function than most people will ever find, much less use frequently. The promise of paying your bills electronically, electronic banking, email, and an endless source of information from the Internet is still not enough to lure a large portion of the population into the computer domain. We have heard for years the term *information appliance* and have promoted the concept as a sort of Holy Grail for interface design. Perhaps the new wave of hybrid television-PCs, Web-oriented televisions, set-top boxes, and Internet-connected home appliances will validate this direction. But what are the key issues that such designs address, and are the solutions applicable to the more general-purpose realm of personal computing?

The Problems of User Interface Design

The industry has been at the task of graphical interface design for more than a decade now, with only incremental improvements in evidence. If we believe that ease-of-use is a major contributor to long-term acceptance of computer technology, we have to make orders of magnitude improvements in our designs and methodologies. We can no longer rely on hand-picked teams of craftspersons and artists, highly trained and experienced multidisciplinary teams of experts, to create compelling and productive products. There simply aren't enough of these skilled people available, and it takes too long to train them, especially since the training is primarily based on experience. We must begin to focus these skills on creating methodologies and tools that can be employed by a larger number of designers. We must create methodologies and tools that can be learned easily, that don't require years of background in the field, and that embody the principles of user-centered design that we endorse. We must leverage the skills of the few to both enable and benefit the expanding marketplace. OVID accomplishes this by providing a process that guides interface developers to a good, object-oriented design.

Today's personal computer is a collage of hardware and software from a variety of suppliers. Although the industry expends great effort to standardize hardware and software interfaces and make configuration automatic using approaches such as plug-and-play, these efforts often fall short of controlling the runaway escalation of function and complexity.

Consider the likely number of suppliers involved in creating the overall user experience of any individual PC. On the hardware side there is the BIOS provider, with its CMOS setup interface, and a variety of peripheral suppliers for disk drive adapters, modems, video adapters, and sound cards—all with their own BIOS, setup, and configuration idiosyncrasies, which aren't supposed to be visible to end users but usually turn out to be visible in some unappreciated way.

Hardware interface and compatibility standards have traditionally been precisely specified, resulting in a fairly reliable user experience. Except for having to plug jumpers or set DIP switches, the user experience in installing a new hardware device used to be relatively reliable. However, with the explosion of new standards, such as the evolution of the bus from ISA to EISA, VESA, PCI, and USB; video adapters ranging from CGA, EGA, VGA, SVGA (in several versions), and now MPEG compatible; along with the sometimes unpredictable "plug-and-pray" capability, the user faces an ever more daunting experience of hardware incompatibility any time a system component is upgraded or otherwise changed.

On the software side it is even more of a free-for-all. There are the operating system, device drivers, installation and configuration programs, and finally the applications the user is actually interested in. Some programs provide an uninstall capability, but many of those have bugs that leave bits and pieces strewn throughout your hard file. Woe to the user who likes to try new programs frequently. You might as well set aside a separate hard file or partition that can be periodically formatted, but, even then, who knows what residue is left over in the system directories? Software is far too difficult to install, administer, and use.

Even highly skilled computer professionals who use computers extensively throughout their day frequently experience daunting and perplexing situations that take hours or even days to resolve.

Fortunately, most of these incidents result only in the loss of time and productivity, and increased stress and frustration on the part of the user. However, too frequently computer interface glitches result in a loss of data and, in some extreme cases, the loss of life. In his book *Set Phasers on Stun*, Steven Casey (1993) documents chilling examples of computer interfaces gone awry. His introduction succinctly states why an increased focus on interface design is becoming of paramount importance to the industry:

> Human errors account for a growing share of death and misfortune in our skies, waterways, workplaces, and hospitals. Structurally sound aircraft plummet to the earth, ships run aground in calm seas, industrial machines run awry, and the instruments of medical science maim and kill unsuspecting patients, all because of incompatibilities between the way things are designed and the way people perceive, think, and act. New technologies will succeed or fail based on our ability to minimize these incompatibilities between the characteristics of people and the characteristics of the things we create and use.

In one particular incident documented in Casey's book, a radiation therapy patient was killed as the result of a malfunctioning machine and a confusing computer interface, which caused the technician to repeatedly administer lethal doses of radiation. OVID provides checks to make sure the interface is complete and understandable to users.

Fortunately, most of the anecdotes that we exchange daily are not so lethal, but each of us has our favorite stories of interface design gone awry or apparently ignored altogether. Throughout the industry, and more than ever before from users themselves, we are beginning to hear pleas for simplification—a reversal of the direction from ever-increasing function and complexity.

The need for simplification is becoming widely recognized, as evidenced in the popular press by articles such as the *Wall Street Journal*'s "Computer Makers Take Note: Cut the Glitz, Keep It Simple" (Mossberg 1996); a *Business Week* special report titled "The Race Is on to Simplify," which stated that "pulling the unwired masses into the Information Age means gadgets must be as easy to use as the telephone" (Sager et al. 1996); and "One Step Forward, Two Steps Back with IBM," published in the *New York Times* (Manes 1996). Each of these articles addresses the complexities and bewildering variety of functions that are thrust on unsuspecting and unsophisticated computer users. The problem is well recognized by almost everyone in the user community! It is not as readily acknowledged by many developers within the industry.

Why is it that systems, especially those that rely heavily on software, continue to experience such a high degree of ease-of-use problems? Brooks (1986) believes that "the hard part of building software is the specification, design, and testing of this conceptual construct, not the labor of representing it and testing the fidelity of the representation." He points out that software systems have orders of more magnitude states than computers do and that in most cases, the elements interact with each other in some nonlinear fashion, and the complexity of the whole function increases much more than linearly. Brooks writes, "From the complexity comes the difficulty of communication among team members, product flaws, cost overruns, and schedule delays."

Complexity makes it difficult to enumerate all the states, which contributes to unreliability. It also makes programs difficult to use and difficult to extend without the addition of unanticipated side effects and security loopholes. OVID breaks software development into manageable steps.

Brooks sees advancements in requirements refinement and rapid prototyping as one of the most promising developments: "Therefore, one of the most promising of the current technological efforts, and one that attacks the essence, not the accidents, of the software problem, is the development of approaches and tools for rapid prototyping of systems, as prototyping is part of the iterative specification of requirements." OVID makes use of prototypes for testing and communicating design. He concludes that "the most important single effort we can mount is to develop ways to grow great designers." Although OVID won't do that by itself, we believe that it is a superb tool to raise the productivity level of every designer who embraces it.

User interface design approaches currently are prone to several types of errors. These errors typically include omissions and ambiguities, which lead to miscommunication, especially between designers and implementors. Designers have an obligation to users. They are obliged to provide functions that are useful, efficient, and easily learned. In order to do so they must understand users' requirements, skills, and motivations. But an excellent design is only worthwhile if the implementation is faithful. The design must not only be complete and precise, it must be communicated accurately to the implementors.

When the interface designer has failed to completely specify all conditions, decisions are left to the implementors, who typically do not have the background in understanding users and their tasks that is necessary to specify an appropriate response to users' actions. Implementors are tempted to make design decisions based on ease of coding rather than user needs.

When the design fails to account for all actions a user might attempt to perform, even actions that might be deemed illogical by the designer, the system response will be dictated by the implementation—without the benefit of thoughtful analysis by the interface designer.

Enter OVID

The strength of the OVID (Object, View, and Interaction Design) methodology is that it provides a complete and thorough specification of the user interface, in a form that is well suited to iterative design and team communication. Through the use of a rigorous approach to analyzing and extracting information from task analysis, designers can construct an accurate, extendible, conceptual model that closely matches users' existing concepts and presents new function, in a well-integrated manner. It is appropriate, therefore, that the acronym OVID alludes to the poet Ovid, whose *Metamorphoses* describes creation and change according to a grand design:

> Of bodies chang'd to various forms, I sing:
> Ye Gods, from whom these miracles did spring,
> Inspire my numbers with celestial heat;
> 'Till I my long laborious work compleat:
> And add perpetual tenour to my rhymes,
> Deduc'd from Nature's birth, to Caesar's times.

—Ovid, *Metamorphoses*

OVID is the first interface design methodology that incorporates all these characteristics, along with the ability to use currently popular object-oriented analysis and design tools, such as Rational Rose.

This approach has been developed specifically for user interface designers. In this book we address the steps of interface design from task analysis through the communication of the intended design to implementors. We do not specify a particular task analysis approach, because many such approaches are well documented in the literature.

OVID addresses the steps of interface design, beginning with analysis and decomposition of tasks from the task analysis. The primary goal is the creation of a precise and complete object model that describes all concepts necessary for complete user understanding of the product. This model includes descriptions of the objects users will employ to perform their tasks, the properties of those objects, and the inter-relationships between them.

This model, called the *designer's model*, encapsulates all aspects of the product in terms appropriate to end users. Aspects specific to an implementation are omitted. The designer's model provides a vehicle for early design sessions involving users and subsequent iteration through product development. Completeness criteria and measurements are an inherent aspect.

The designer's model is presented to users in the form of one or more views, each of which implements some subset of the tasks to be performed. Within each view the supported tasks are mapped to user interactions using available input/output mechanisms, such as pointing devices, keyboards, and voice recognition. The result is a finely woven specification for an overall user experience, through which team members can trace, test, and verify individual threads. Objects, views, and interactions are choreographed with each other to support the tasks users need to perform.

The practice of user-interface (UI) design today is more art than science. UI design is usually done ad hoc—with no particular methodology. There is no consistent technique for documenting and communicating the interface design. Designs are often incomplete, forcing the programmers to make design decisions when they implement. There are often features in the design that can't be implemented. The interface design is usually not specified in a form that is easy for the programming team to translate into code. The result is that the product often ends up with an interface different from what the UI designer intended. When this happens, much time and effort has been wasted.

Object-oriented program design, on the other hand, is generally practiced using methodologies that have proven to be very successful. These methodologies include Booch, Schlaer-Mellor, Rumbaugh, and OMT. Unfortunately, these methodologies do not adequately address user-interface design.

OVID combines the best of both camps. We use the notation and modeling techniques of successful code design methodologies and combine these with the processes that UI designers were already doing well, such as user requirements gathering, prototyping, and usability testing. OVID brings structure to the design process to lead the designer to a good, object-oriented design. It coordinates the effort of multidisciplinary design teams. It makes use of design tools to increase design efficiency. It provides checks for design completeness that help to prevent design errors and reduce iteration. OVID is independent of implementation platform. OVID brings rigor to UI design and produces output that feeds directly into code design. It begins the transformation of the UI design process from art to science.

The Structure of This Book

This book has four major parts:

- Part I describes the foundations on which OVID is based. It describes object-oriented user interfaces, the models on which we base our interfaces, and the object-oriented user interface development process into which OVID fits.

- Part II provides the OVID methodology for designing user interfaces. It covers customer requirements collection, model construction, design, and implementation.

- Part III describes prototyping and testing—the key supporting tasks of OVID.

- Part IV presents information that will help you learn more about OVID, including a case study, exercises, a glossary, and a bibliography.

The notational conventions in this book are from the Unified Modeling Language (UML), and examples were created using the Rational Rose modeling tool. These are not required to practice OVID—you can use another notation or tool if you prefer.

How to Use This Book

We understand that people will use this book in different ways. We have organized it in a modular fashion, so that you can read just parts or vary the order in which you read the chapters to match your interests and time constraints.

If you are unfamiliar with the theory behind object-oriented user interfaces, you should read Part I. If you are unfamiliar with user-centered design of software systems, you should read Part III. Everyone should read Part II because this is the core of the OVID methodology and is different from any other interface design or software development methodology. Part II is the material you will need to refer to frequently as you practice OVID for the first time. Read Part IV if you would like to practice using the OVID design techniques.

PART I

Foundations

CHAPTER 1

What Is an Object-Oriented User Interface?

- **Objects**
  Objects are the main component of the object-oriented user interface, which allows users to organize the information in the computer environment similarly to the way they organize objects in the real world.

- **Classes**
  Object classes are objects that share similar behaviors and characteristics.

- **Instances**
  Each object the user interacts with is an *instance*, or unique occurrence, of an object class.

- **Views**
  Views present information to users and allow them to use the information to accomplish desired tasks.

An object-oriented user interface focuses the user on objects—the "things" people use to accomplish their work. Users see and manipulate object representations of their information. Each different kind of object supports actions appropriate for the information it represents. Users of object-oriented computer user interfaces need not be aware of computer programs and underlying computer technology in order to use computers.

Although many of their concepts are similar, object-oriented programming (OOP) and object-oriented user interfaces (OOUI) aren't the same thing. Simply using an OO language does not guarantee an OOUI; as a matter of fact, you don't have to use an OO language to create an OOUI, but it helps. Because the concepts involved are similar, the two disciplines can be used in a complementary relationship. The primary distinction that designers and programmers must keep in mind is that OOUI design concentrates on objects *that are perceived by users*. OO programming focuses on implementation details that often need to be hidden from the user.

In OOUI design, different kinds of objects are said to belong to different *classes*. Class distinctions are based on behaviors that are common within a group of objects and that differ between groups of objects (for example, a folder is a class of object that can be used to contain other objects). Memos, reports, graphs, and movies are examples of other kinds of objects that might be grouped together in a folder. Folders are distinctly different from other kinds of objects, but all folders exhibit similar appearance and behavioral characteristics. They are all members of the folder class.

Specialization can be achieved by defining *subclasses*; for example, a portfolio that automatically arranges specific kinds of objects into sections could be designed as a subclass of the folder class. The folder is a general-purpose container, which can contain objects of many different classes. To use a folder, the user learns the properties and behaviors of folders. These properties and behaviors are designed to support the addition of new objects to the folder, arranging the objects in the folder, and viewing the folder's contents (the folder's primary tasks).

The portfolio, a specialization, is a subclass of the folder class. A subclass *inherits* properties and behaviors from its parent class. New properties and behaviors are added to the subclass by the developer to create the desired specialization. Because the portfolio inherits the properties and behaviors of the folder, users can transfer their knowledge of the folder to the portfolio. They need only learn the distinguishing features of the portfolio to take advantage of its intended benefits.

The object classes and subclasses that are seen by users should be derived directly from analysis of the users' tasks and understanding the users' goals, motivations, and current techniques. In this way the objects presented through the computer interface will be more easily recognized and their roles more readily understood.

In general, objects are composed of and contain other objects—that is, objects are composed of other objects, which in turn are made up of yet other objects—all the way down to elemental objects, which cannot be further decomposed by the user. The *composition* of an object contributes to its class membership and therefore to establishing its properties and behaviors. Many kinds of objects are also *containers* of other objects. The distinction between composition and containment is often quite clear and useful, but in some cases the line can become blurred. That is when designers must rely on task analysis to help answer questions about the usefulness of certain distinctions as perceived by users.

Users interact with objects through *views*, which present information and support interaction through the various input/output devices of the computer. Typical user tasks involve working with a variety of object properties, using various object behaviors, and working with several objects at the same time. In practice it is rarely possible to support all necessary tasks using a single view of an object. Objects typically must provide multiple views, each specialized for a specific set of tasks.

> **Note**
>
> *We use the term view to include all presentation forms, including nonvisual forms such as audio.*

The basis of Object, View, and Interaction Design (OVID) is a methodical analysis and design approach to identifying objects, defining views for sets of desired tasks, and specifying the interaction techniques used within each view to accomplish the intended tasks. OVID is an ideal methodology to use when designing an object-oriented user interface. With OVID, an interface designer can identify objects that make the users' tasks most efficient.

An OOUI enables a user to focus on objects and work with them directly, which more closely reflects the user's real-world way of doing work. This is in contrast to the traditional application-oriented interface, in which the users must find a program appropriate for both the task they want to perform and the type of information they want to use. Then they must start the program and use some mechanism provided by the program, such as an Open dialog box, to locate the information and use it.

If you are familiar with the concepts of object-oriented programming, you will have noticed quite a few similarities and common terms. Keep in mind that the major distinction is *user orientation*. OOUI design is concerned with users' perceptions—the concepts and techniques that users find necessary or useful in accomplishing their tasks. OOUI design seeks to hide those implementation aspects that are not relevant to users' tasks.

The following sections present a more in-depth description of OOUI concepts.

1.1 Objects

An *object* is something a user needs to work with to perform a task. It is any entity that can be manipulated as a unit or that can be thought of by a user as capable of existing independently. A spreadsheet, a cell in a spreadsheet, a bar chart, a title in a bar chart, a report, a telephone number, a folder, a printer, a word or sentence, and even a single character are examples of objects. Each of us deals with objects daily. Some objects, such as telephones, are so common that we find them in many places. Other objects, such as the folders in a file cabinet or the tools we use for home repairs, may be located in certain places.

An object-oriented user interface allows users to organize objects in the computer environment similarly to the way they organize objects in the real world. Users can keep objects used across many tasks in a common, convenient place, and they can keep objects used for specific tasks in more specific places.

Task analysis provides the basis for identifying user objects. For example, in the design of an object-oriented car dealership application, some of the objects identified might include

- A worksheet containing the details about a car that a customer wants to buy
- A customer description containing information about the customer
- A car lot providing a list of the new cars in stock
- Pictures and text describing the cars in stock and those that can be ordered
- A work area grouping all the objects needed during the task of selling a car
- A printer for printing the worksheet
- In-baskets and out-baskets for communicating with the sales and finance managers

In traditional graphical user interfaces, objects are typically represented on a user's screen as *icons*. Icons are small graphic images that help a user identify an object. They typically consist of a picture, which conveys the object's class, and a text title, which identifies the specific object. Icons are intended to provide a concise, easy-to-manipulate representation of an object regardless of how much additional information the object may contain. If desired, a user can open an icon to see a view of this additional information.

Users can perform actions on icons using various techniques, such as point-select, choosing an action from a menu, and drag and drop.

In the future, objects may be depicted using more realistic presentation approaches (for example, using 3D graphics). A real-world appearance could prove very useful for helping new users become comfortable using a computer. Objects that look and behave in a realistic manner would be immediately recognizable and intuitive to use.

1.2 Classes

Object classes are used to distinguish one type of object from another. Object classes are very useful because they help designers make clear distinctions between the types of objects that their products need to provide. These distinctions, in turn, make it easy for users to learn and predict how an object will behave and therefore how they can use it to accomplish their tasks. The distinctions that allow objects to be grouped into classes are their characteristics and uses or, to use OOUI terminology, their *properties* and *behaviors*.

Different properties and behaviors are used as the basis for making distinctions between classes and subclasses. The basis for distinction must be clearly defined and relevant to the users of the objects. This is easy to see when parallels are drawn between computer objects and objects that are found in the world in general—for example, automobile could be a class that includes properties such as body style, price range, and optimizations for intended uses, among others. Subclasses of automobiles might include full-size, compact, luxury, and sports car.

An object-oriented user interface defines a class hierarchy for user objects. Data, for example, is a class that includes document, chart, and picture as subclasses. The class hierarchy for vehicles, for example, might look as shown in Figure 1.1.

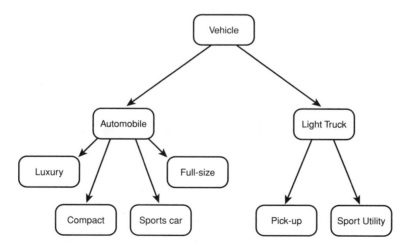

FIGURE 1.1 *A class hierarchy for vehicles.*

1.3 Instances

Each object the user interacts with is an *instance,* or unique occurrence, of an object class. The automobiles on a car dealer's lot are instances of the luxury, full-size, compact, and sports car subclasses—just as a specific memo is an instance of the document subclass of data.

Just as the real cars on a car dealership's lot are instances of automobiles, the icons of cars that could be shown in a computerized version of the dealer's lot represent instances. Each instance of a class has the same properties: year, make, model, and so forth. Also, each instance follows the same rules of behavior. An action performed on one of these instances, such as changing the price, could be performed on any other instance of the same class.

Icons help to depict the class of an object by providing a pictorial representation— for example, icons help a user to see that the objects in a list belong to the automo- bile class. A logical next step is for the icon of an instance to present properties and behaviors that reflect the current state of that instance. Interactive icons that present useful information about an object and allow users to interact with it provide signif- icant added value over the inanimate placeholders so often used today. Ultimately the use of icons will give way to realistic presentations of objects that are not limited to the size and shape constraints of icons. The use of images in Web pages is already setting a new direction. These images can be fully interactive compositions resem- bling things users are already familiar with, making interaction more intuitive than ever.

Although users create and manipulate objects, many users will never have to be consciously aware of which class an object belongs to. For example, a person approaching an office chair does not need to stop and think, "This is an office chair, which belongs to the class chair. Therefore, I can sit on it." Likewise, a user can work with charts and come to expect that all charts will behave in the same way without caring that the charts are a subclass of the data object class.

Object classes are also very useful to product designers because they prompt design- ers to think about making clear distinctions among the classes of objects that should be provided for the user. Object classes must be carefully defined with respect to tasks and distinctions that users currently understand and that are useful. Carefully defining and clearly distinguishing object classes enables users to learn and predict the behavior of objects.

1.4 Composition and Containment

The *composition* of an object is important for understanding its design and should not be confused with *containment*. All objects except the most elemental ones are composed of and may contain other objects; for example, a spreadsheet is an object that is composed of cells, and cells are objects that can contain text, mathematical formulas, video, and so forth. The breaking down of objects into the objects from which they are composed is called *decomposition*.

A useful distinction between composition and containment can be understood through a comparison of different kinds of vehicles. Take, for instance, the differences between cars and trucks. The task-based intent of the two classes is fairly clear: A car is for carrying people; a truck is for carrying things. Granted, a car can carry things (that's what the trunk is for) and a truck can carry people, but the designs of the two vehicles are optimized for the primary tasks of carrying people or things. A car is much more comfortable for the passengers than a truck, where the passengers must ride in the cargo area.

Now what makes a car a *car* and a truck a *truck* are differences in composition that provide the task optimizations that we find useful. Cars have comfortable seats, multiple doors for easy entry, air conditioning, and six-speaker surround-sound stereo for everyone. Trucks have large, flat cargo areas with hydraulic lifts and tie-downs. There is certainly some overlap in the composition of cars and trucks—both may provide similar comforts for the driver—but there are striking differences that cause us to classify and use them differently. These differences are reflected in the *composition* of each class—the set of components from which each is constructed.

On the other hand, both cars and trucks are containers. They can contain people, plants, dogs, and packages. What is important is that what is contained at any point in time has no impact on the vehicle's classification as a car or a truck—in other words, while an object's design (composition) might be optimized to facilitate containment of certain things, what it actually contains has little bearing on what kind of object it is. The importance of this distinction to the designer is that users might be allowed to alter the composition of an object to some degree—to fine-tune the optimizations, for example—but typically do not transmute one object into another, and separate views and interaction techniques are often appropriate to optimize and distinguish containment tasks from composition tasks.

The depth to which object decomposition should be supported in the interface depends entirely on what a user finds practical or useful in performing a particular task. A user who is writing a report, for example, would probably not be interested in dealing with objects smaller than characters, so in this task characters would be elemental objects. However, a user who is creating or editing a character font might need to manipulate individual pixels or strokes. In this task, characters would be composed of pixels or strokes and therefore a character would not be an elemental object.

1.5 Views

Object *views* present information to users and allow them to use the information to accomplish desired tasks. The set of tasks that users need to perform can be quite large, so they are typically grouped into sets of related subtasks, which are then enabled through several views.

Composition and containment tasks are two of the most common sets of tasks and are therefore the basis of a fundamental view-type distinction. Views can generally be classified as composed, contents, properties, and user assistance or help. Composed views present information as a composition, combining multiple elements into a single overall presentation; for example, a print preview, which combines body text with headers and footers in a word processor, is a composed view. If a word processor allows multiple different files to be included into a final form document, it might provide a listing of all the files to be included. This would be a contents view. Folders are the most obvious objects that provide contents views. Folders don't provide composed views because they are general-purpose containers. There is no relationship among the contents of a folder that would be depicted in a composed view. However, a subclass of folder that contained, for example, all the pages of a document on the World Wide Web, might very well provide a composed view of the document. (See Figures 1.2 through 1.5.)

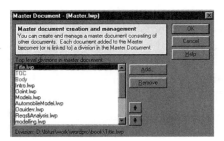

FIGURE 1.2 *A contents view.*

Property views show the properties of an object, and user assistance views provide help, tutorials, and other useful information about using the object. You might recognize this general design paradigm. It has been implemented to some degree on both IBM's OS/2 Warp and Microsoft's Windows 95 platforms.

Again, the importance to the designer is in identifying the need for these different classes of views based on task analysis, deciding the subset of tasks to be supported by each view, and enabling the tasks through interaction techniques using the various input/output devices available. That's what OVID is all about.

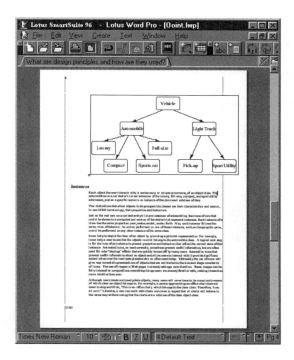

FIGURE 1.3   *A composed view.*

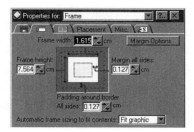

FIGURE 1.4   *A properties view.*

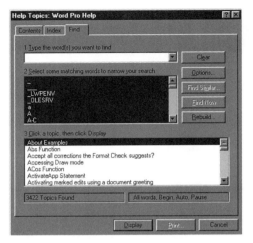

Figure 1.5 *A user assistance view.*

1.6 Benefits of Using an OOUI

An OOUI lessens the need for users to be aware of the implementation. Instead, users can concentrate on locating the information needed to accomplish their tasks and on using that information. Aspects of starting and running programs can be hidden to all but those users who want to be aware of them. In many enterprise environments, tasks such as setup and configuration are performed by users who have been given specialized training. A typical user should only need to know which objects are required to perform his or her tasks and how to use those objects to achieve desired results.

By eliminating computer-oriented aspects such as starting and running programs, the learning process for each user is simplified. The learning process is further simplified because the user has only one process to deal with—viewing an object—as opposed to starting an application and then finding and opening or creating a file. A computer is a tool and, as with any other tool, it has to be learned to be used effectively. However, when we can help a user by simplifying the process of learning to use a tool, we should do so.

An implicit benefit of using an OOUI is that designers have to think more explicitly about distinctions between object classes that are useful to users. Each object class provided in a product should be distinctly different from other object classes in a way that users find natural, easy to remember, and useful. The more similar object classes are, the harder it is for a user to comprehend their differences. Therefore, designers should provide obvious and useful distinctions so that object classes and behaviors are well matched to the users' tasks. A thorough analysis of users' tasks, goals, and motivations is indispensable in this endeavor.

CHAPTER **2**

User Interface Design Models

- **The users' conceptual models**
  The users' conceptual models of a system are mental images that each user subconsciously forms through experience.

- **The designer's model**
  The designer's model represents the designer's intent in terms of objects users will see and how they will use the objects to accomplish their tasks.

- **The programmer's model**
  The programmer's model describes the system internals used to implement the designer's model.

- **Reconciling the models**
  It is crucial that all three models be considered when designing object-oriented user interfaces. Otherwise, the interface is not usable in the real world.

Models are used in many different fields. Researchers in physics, chemistry, and molecular biology use models to explore relationships between atomic and molecular components of systems. Economists and city planners use models to analyze and predict the performance of complex economic and social systems. Teachers use models as an aid in explaining complex systems in a variety of fields. Whether the model is a plastic replica of an airplane, an exploded parts diagram in a book, or an elaborate computer simulation, the purpose of the model is to convey an understanding of the components that make up an object or a system and relationships between components. Figure 2.1 illustrates the components that make up a radio receiver and an automobile.

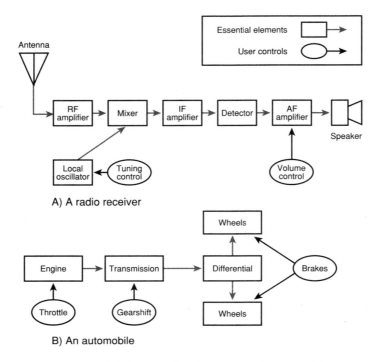

FIGURE 2.1 *Block diagrams of a radio receiver and an automobile.*

Models can be useful in designing and analyzing the user interface (UI) of a computer system. Relationships between elements in the interface, the programming system that implements the elements, and the users of the interface can be described and analyzed by using models. Furthermore, a model of the interface can be implemented as a prototype to support iterative testing with users.

In user interface design we use models to describe an interface in terms of objects, properties, behaviors, and relationships between objects. A model provides a framework for communication, understanding, and decision making. Three models (see Figure 2.2) are relevant to the design and implementation of a user interface. Each model provides a different perspective on the interface, beginning with the user's perspective and including the designer's perspective and the implementing programmer's perspective.

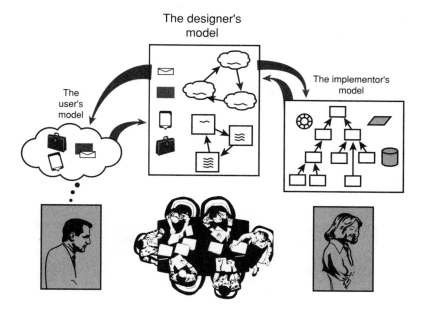

FIGURE 2.2   *Three models relevant to the design and implementation of user interfaces.*

A model does not need to address every aspect and feature of a system. A level of detail adequate to understand relationships of interest, explain observations, and make design tradeoffs is sufficient. In some cases it may be desirable to use several different models with various levels of detail for the same system. One model might be adequate for a salesperson to explain the system to a prospective customer. Another model of the system might be needed to help develop specifications for subcontracted components.

A model must be accurate at whatever level of detail is chosen. Models must be under constant scrutiny and should be changed to reflect varying requirements and explain observed behaviors.

We have found it useful to consider three models during user interface design:

- The *users' conceptual models,* which represent what the users think is happening and why

- The user interface *designer's model*, which describes what the user is intended to experience

- The *programmer's model*, which describes implementation details

Although the details of these models as described here are specific to an object-oriented user interface, the use of these models and the relationships among them apply to the design of user interfaces in general.

To illustrate the relationship between these three models, consider an analogy between the role of a user interface designer and an architect who is designing a house. These roles are similar in many respects because both of them require an understanding of all three models.

The user interface designer's role is to create a designer's model, or blueprint, of the user interface—just as an architect creates a blueprint of a house. To do this, the designer must:

- Understand the user's conceptual model. Just as an architect must understand a client's needs and expectations to design a house that pleases the client, the user interface designer needs to understand users, their tasks, and their expectations.

- Use accepted user interface design principles. Architects use basic principles that apply to housing design. A good architect knows the environment in which the house will be built with regard to temperature, weather, humidity, and other factors, as well as successful designs that have been used in that environment. Accordingly, the user interface designer needs to have a knowledge of accepted and proven principles in the field of user interface design.

- Understand the capabilities and limitations of the programming environment and the skills of the programmers who will be implementing the interface. Just as an architect must know the strengths and weaknesses of building materials and the skills of the tradespeople who will build the house, user interface designers must understand the capabilities and restrictions of operating systems, file systems, window managers, programming toolkits, and other components used to implement the interface.

- Create a designer's model (blueprint) that reflects the architect's understanding of all these requirements.

2.1 The Users' Conceptual Models

The *users' conceptual models* of a system are mental images that each user subconsciously forms as he or she interacts with the system (see Figure 2.3). People create mental models by putting together sets of perceived rules and patterns in a way that explains a situation. A typical person cannot draw or describe his or her mental models. This is not to say that a person cannot state or write requirements for a system, but he or she may be unable to describe the model of how the system works. In many situations a person is not even aware that these mental models exist.

A mental model does not necessarily reflect a situation and its components accurately. It is based on a user's *perceptions*, which are not always accurate interpretations of reality. Still, a mental model can help people predict what will happen next in a given situation, and it serves as a framework for analysis, understanding, and decision making.

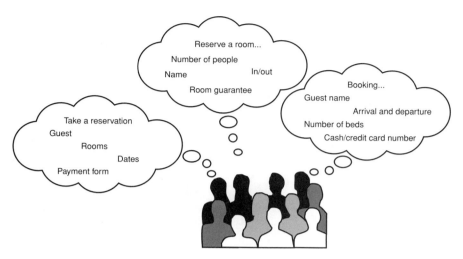

FIGURE 2.3 *Users' conceptual models.*

The user's conceptual model is based on each user's expectations and understanding of what a system provides in terms of functions and objects, how the system responds when the user interacts with it, and the goals the user wants to accomplish during that interaction. These expectations, understandings, and goals are influenced by the user's experiences, including interaction with other systems, such as typewriters, calculators, and video games.

Because each user's conceptual model is influenced by different experiences, users' models often differ. Each user looks at a user interface from a slightly different perspective.

The problem for the interface designer is to design an interface that users find predictable and intuitive when each user is approaching the interface from a different perspective. To come as close as possible to matching users' conceptual models, designers should find out as much as they can about users' skills and motivations, the tasks they perform, and their expectations. This process involves:

- Using resources such as task analysis, surveys, customer visits, and user requirements lists

- Incorporating information that users provide into the user interface design

- Conducting usability tests

This is an iterative process, which may require many cycles. As the design progresses, users may identify aspects of the interface that are difficult to learn, that are counterproductive, or that they simply do not like.

Through interaction with the user interface, users' conceptual models may be expanded, which in turn may cause users to realize new requirements that they had not thought of before. As users provide this level of information to the designer, the picture of their conceptual models will become clearer.

Conceptual models of an object-oriented user interface (OOUI) consist of the objects, properties, behaviors, and relationships of those objects that are involved in the user's interaction with the system.

When a user first interacts with a new interface, he or she is likely to attempt to understand its operation in terms of roles and relationships he or she already understands. In other words, we each carry with us a current conceptual model. Where existing models lead to correct expectations, the model is reinforced and the user will feel the interface is intuitive. When results are not as expected, the user may rationalize by inventing new rules and relationships in the model in order to explain observed behavior.

If the user-supplied extensions are accurate, they will be reinforced through interaction with similar aspects in different parts of the system. Otherwise, they are likely to cause confusion. Sometimes users develop superstitions about the interface. These superstitions result from incorrect rationalizations about how and why the interface appears to behave as it does. Superstitions are likely to cause unexpected results in response to the user's actions and further contradict the user's intuition. This can lead to a breakdown in understanding and trust by the user. The use of metaphors and consistency by designers can help users correct and extend their conceptual models.

A new interface should resemble something familiar to help users get started and then allow them to explore new concepts. It is often said that a characteristic of a good user interface is that it is *intuitive*. When used in this sense, *intuition* can best be characterized as a good match between the user's conceptual model and the designer's model.

By using metaphors, designers can take advantage of users' experiences and allow users to rely on intuition while expanding the conceptual model to take advantage of new capabilities provided by the interface. Interfaces that use metaphors and allow users to safely explore the computerized environment are popular for this reason—for example, a computerized car dealer application might provide a worksheet object to be used by a salesperson in the task of selling a car. The computerized worksheet would contain the same information and would be used in the same way as a paper worksheet. Like the paper worksheet, the worksheet object would allow the salesperson to enter the car's price and stock number, the customer's name and address, and information about the proposed terms of the sale.

However, the computer-based worksheet could also expand the salesperson's conceptual model by providing capabilities that go beyond those of a paper worksheet. Instead of typing information into the worksheet one field at a time, the salesperson might simply drag and drop a car object onto the worksheet. The fields in the worksheet that are relevant for the car being sold would be automatically filled in by the associated fields from the car object. Monthly payments and finance charges could be calculated automatically. Instead of having to hand a paper worksheet to the sales manager for approval, the salesperson could drag and drop the worksheet into a specific mail out-basket to have it automatically sent to the sales manager through the dealer's computer network.

This worksheet object would not only meet the salesperson's expectations, it would go beyond them. It is an object that the salesperson expects to use during the task of selling a car, it has behaviors and characteristics that the salesperson is accustomed to, and it provides additional value through the use of a computer.

In this example, the worksheet object acts as a metaphor for an object that already exists in the salesperson's conceptual model of a car dealership and the task of selling cars. It is an object with which the salesperson is already comfortable, yet it provides additional capabilities that make the salesperson's job easier than using a paper counterpart.

Users' conceptual models constantly evolve as they interact with an interface. Just as users influence the design of a product, the interface design influences and modifies users' concepts of the system. Designers can help users develop an accurate conceptual model by using well-defined distinctions between objects and by being consistent across all aspects of the interface—for example, given an object-oriented car dealer application, the salesperson would open and work with familiar objects, instead of starting and running computer programs, opening files, and so forth. This object-oriented approach has fewer concepts for the salesperson to deal with and matches the salesperson's real world better than one in which a task is accomplished by starting applications and opening files.

The conceptual model of a salesperson who is already familiar with using a graphical computer interface may require little modification. This salesperson would already know how to use icons, windows, menu bars, and pushbuttons.

In any case, the distinctions between objects must be clear and useful, and the interface must be consistent. Otherwise, the users' conceptual models will be modified in ways other than those intended by the interface designer.

2.2 The Designer's Model

The interface components and relationships intended to be seen by users and intended to become part of each user's conceptual model are described in the *designer's model*. This model represents the designer's intent in terms of objects users will see and how they will use the objects to accomplish their tasks. (See Figure 2.4.)

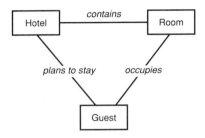

F IGURE 2.4 *A designer's model for a hotel.*

The designer's model identifies objects, how those objects are represented to users (views), and how users interact with those objects using the views. User-oriented objects are defined in terms of properties, behaviors, and relationships with other objects. Differences in properties and behaviors are the basis for class distinctions, such as the distinctions between folders and documents. Relationships between objects affect how they are used in accomplishing users' tasks; for example, users can use folders to contain and organize memos, reports, charts, tables, and many other classes of objects. Users can discard an object by dragging and dropping the object's icon on a wastebasket icon, and users can print an object by dropping the object's icon on a printer icon. These actions are logical in that they maintain real–world relationships between objects.

Traditionally, the user interface of a product has been considered to be the look–and–feel aspects of the product. More recently, the emphasis has been shifting to the *objects* needed by users to accomplish their tasks. This is the basis of an OOUI. Another perspective of the designer's model is given in Section 2.6, "The Designer's Model and the Iceberg Analogy of Usability," in which the look–and–feel aspects of the interface constitute the "tip of the iceberg," and the most important aspects are encapsulated in the object model. An *object model* describes objects, properties, behaviors, and relationships intended to be seen and used by users of the interface. The object model is the main component of the designer's model in an OOUI. The look–and–feel aspects play a supporting role.

By relying on a few basic classes and relationships, with well-defined distinctions based on user task needs, the designer's model should be easy for users to learn and understand. Users should quickly develop conceptual models that closely match the designer's model. (See Figure 2.5.)

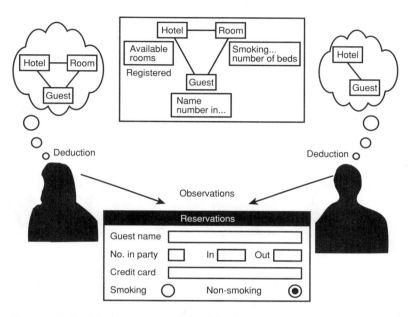

FIGURE 2.5 *Matching users' models and the designer's model.*

The models underlying both IBM's OS/2 Warp and Microsoft's Windows 95 are examples of OOUIs. These models define objects that are common to many types of applications. Product designers add objects that are needed by specific products. This is typically done by extending existing objects (creating subclasses) or by defining entirely new types of objects (creating new classes). Definition of the designer's model is crucial to developing products that are easy to learn and understand. Its definition should comprise the first series of steps during product design.

If the designer's model closely matches a user's conceptual model, the user should learn quickly and apply knowledge correctly in new situations. In other words, the user will feel that the interface is intuitive. Designers can help users to develop a closely matching conceptual model by creating a clear and concise designer's model. A designer's model is clear and concise when it has made a minimum number of distinctions among objects, when the distinctions are clear and useful to users, and when the distinctions are consistently conveyed throughout the interface.

For the designer's model to be consistent with the user's conceptual model, the designer must know the users, their tasks, and their expectations. If designers do not understand their users, the interface will not behave as users will expect it to. If the system does not behave as users expect it to, their conceptual models will be different from the designer's model and misunderstandings will occur. Users can lose confidence in the reliability of their conceptual model, and thus in the system itself, when these misunderstandings occur. If users form an incorrect conclusion or a superstition to explain an inconsistency, they may try to apply it elsewhere in the system. This can lead to further misunderstandings and distrust of the system.

Note

A misunderstanding can be caused by inconsistency in an object's behavior resulting from a particular action. For example, if a user learns that double-clicking the mouse button on an object opens a window, and elsewhere in the interface the same action discards an object, the user will quickly learn to distrust the system.

In summary, the designer's model is the model of objects, properties, behaviors, and relationships that the designer intends the user to understand. The designer's goal is that each user's conceptual model exactly matches the designer's model. Users who perceive the interface at this level have a precise understanding of the interface and can take full advantage of the capabilities intended by the design.

2.3 Accommodating Differences between the Designer's and Users' Conceptual Models

Ideally, a designer's model is equivalent to the user's conceptual model, and a product works the way each user expects it to work. However, various factors can lead to differences between the user's conceptual model and the designer's model. Here are some examples:

- Users have different conceptual models resulting from different real-world experiences.

- Implementation constraints can restrict the function of a product to something less than a user expects.

- A computer product can provide useful features that do not have counterparts in the real world or in the user's area of expertise and therefore do not already exist in the user's conceptual model.

When the designer's model does not exactly match the user's conceptual model, the user often feels as if he or she is viewing a product through a haze—not quite seeing or understanding the product. Some components of the product look and behave as the user expects, whereas others seem somewhat different or even foreign. To dispel the haze, a designer should expose a user to the features of a product in a way that helps shape the user's conceptual model in the form of the designer's model. Then the two become equivalent. (See Figure 2.6.)

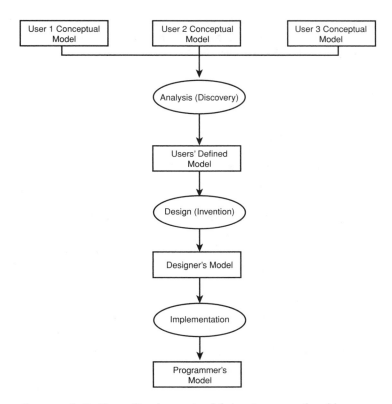

FIGURE 2.6 *Reconciling the users' and designer's conceptual models.*

Consistency and the use of metaphors are helpful for shaping a user's conceptual model. When a new feature is consistent with other, already understood product features, the user can predict the results of using the new feature and can accept the new feature more readily. Likewise, when a new feature is developed around a metaphor for something that exists in a user's conceptual model, a user can make guesses about the new feature by drawing analogies from the familiar concept. The user can then extend the existing conceptual model to incorporate the new feature.

Note

Electronic mail provides an example of a user extending his or her conceptual model to incorporate a new feature. Although most people understand how to mail a letter by using a postal or courier service, few immediately understand how to send information by pressing a key on a keyboard or by placing a computer object on top of another computer object (e.g., placing a document object on top of an out-basket object). By designing this type of information transfer around a mail metaphor, a designer encourages a user to draw on an existing conceptual model, which describes and explains methods for getting information from one place to another. Furthermore, if a designer has specified an interaction technique that is

continues

consistent with other interaction techniques a user is familiar with, a user will be able to extend a conceptual model of mail to include electronic mail. For example, if a user knows how to mail a hard-copy document by placing it into the office out-basket, the user can easily learn to mail a document object by placing it into an out-basket object on a computer.

A designer's model must also be flexible enough to accommodate growing sophistication in users. As users become more proficient in using a product, they might find that they do not like certain aspects of the interface, or they might realize that they want or need functions they had not thought of before. A successful designer anticipates a user's progress and provides mechanisms that are robust enough to expand as novice users become expert users—for example, when working with a printer object, a typical user wants information about which objects are in the printer's queue, as well as the orientation and number of copies the printer will produce. This information should be readily available. However, a more sophisticated user might want information about the printer's connections, baud rate, and communication protocol. This information should also be available, but it should not get in the way of the information needed by a typical user. By layering information, a designer can keep a product's interface free of clutter and can avoid intimidating novice users while still meeting the needs of expert users.

2.4 The Programmer's Model

The *programmer's model* describes the system internals used to implement the designer's model. The programmer's model includes details relevant only to the programmer. For example, the designer's model might include a directory object consisting of people's names, addresses, office numbers, and so forth. The programmer's model of the directory object might consist of records in a file, with one record for each directory entry; or it could be a complex organization of multiple records from multiple files. These implementation details from the programmer's model should not be evident in the designer's model and are therefore not apparent to users. (See Figure 2.7.)

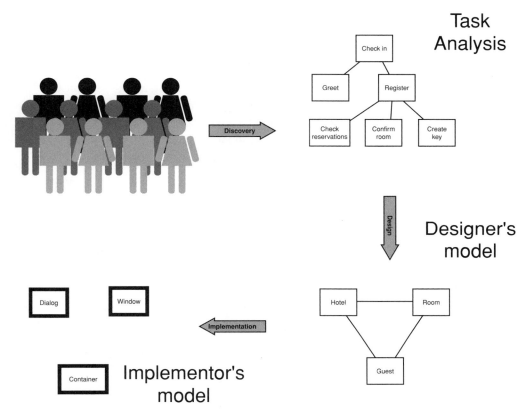

FIGURE 2.7 *The steps leading to development of the programmer's model.*

2.5 Accommodating the Programmer's Model

Ideally, the designer should create a model appropriate for users, and the programmer should write code that supports the designer's entire model. However, the designer usually has to make concessions due to the restrictions of typical programming environments. For example, in a product that offers an electronic mail feature, the designer might specify that the user should receive some kind of immediate notification when mail reaches its intended recipient. But if the network that the mail travels on is subject to unpredictable delays, the designer might have to settle for a notification that arrives as soon as the network allows, rather than an immediate notification. The designer might also have to add a feature that lets the user know where a piece of mail is while en route.

While accommodating the programmer's model, the designer should be certain to shield users from complex details of a product's implementation. Any aspect of a programmer's model that must be exposed to a user must first be filtered through the designer's mode (for example, a typical user expects that the information displayed in a window is up-to-date). The user's expectation should be reflected in the designer's model. However, a programmer cannot always ensure that displayed information is up-to-date; perhaps a network delay interferes. To bridge the gap between a user's expectations and what a programmer can deliver, a designer's model can include a visual indication to the user when the information is out-of-date and provide the user with an interaction technique to refresh the display.

Just as an architect must know the strengths and weaknesses of building materials and the skills of the builders contracted to construct a home, the interface designer must be aware of the capabilities and limitations of the programming environment and the skills of the programmers who will implement the design.

2.6 The Designer's Model and the Iceberg Analogy of Usability

The three main aspects of the designer's model are

- Visual representations (the "look" of the interface)
- Interaction techniques (the "feel" of the interface)
- Objects and their properties, behaviors, and relationships (the object model)

These aspects are depicted in Figures 2.8 and 2.9.

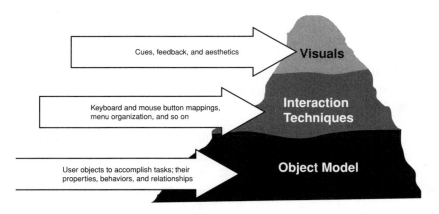

FIGURE 2.8 *The iceberg analogy of the designer's usability model.*

- Toolkits, user interface models, and style guides help with look and feel, the tip of the usability iceberg.

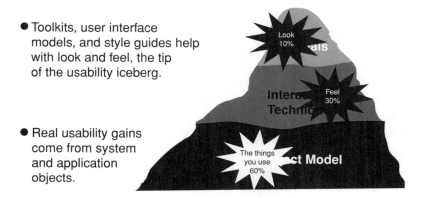

- Real usability gains come from system and application objects.

FIGURE 2.9 *Contributors to usability.*

The visual representations and interaction techniques—the look-and-feel—have traditionally been the most discussed aspects of a user interface. More recently, the object-oriented aspects have been recognized as making the most significant contribution to a product's usability. When a user first uses a computer to perform a task, such as preparing a sales analysis report, he must understand what the computer can do. He must translate his goals into terms the computer supports and understands. The computer may provide tables, graphs, charts, and text entry. These objects have properties the user can modify, such as width, height, color, number of columns, style of graph, and so on. The computer might also support some relationships between objects. For example, it might be able to generate charts and graphs automatically from tables of numbers. Understanding what the objects are and what each of them does is the most important factor in learning how to use the computer to do work. Exactly how the user tells the computer what to do (the look-and-feel aspects) is a secondary consideration. This is roughly analogous to the relationship between language and ideas in communication. We might express an idea in English, German, French, Italian, or Spanish, but the ideas being expressed are the fundamental aspect of communication. In UI design, the objects, object properties, and relationships are the ideas, and the look and feel is the language.

Objects and their relationships are the most important aspects of the designer's model, and a designer should spend a considerable amount of effort defining them. At an early stage of product development, the designer should determine what objects a user requires, what properties and behaviors the objects should have, and what relationships should exist between objects—for example, if a designer were developing a model of a product for a car dealer, he or she might determine that a user, in this case a salesperson, needs a car object and a customer object. The user might also need a worksheet object, in which information from both the car and the customer are combined during the course of selling a car. Finally, the user might need one or more container objects, such as folders and baskets, to contain and organize the objects.

When a designer chooses the objects, their properties, behaviors, and relationships carefully, and accurately matches them to the relationships in the *user's conceptual model*, the visual representations follow naturally.

2.7 Visual Representations

A designer's model also addresses the appearance of objects. The visual appearances of objects should be consistent with one another as well as with other objects in the operating environment. Visual aspects can be categorized as *operational* or *aesthetic*.

The operational aspects of an interface include visual cues and feedback. Visual cues serve to direct and prompt the user's actions. For example, when visual elements are highlighted in some way as the pointer passes over them, the user quickly comes to realize that these elements are active and that some action will occur if they are clicked on. Visual feedback serves to confirm and reassure the user that the action has been recognized. Strictly speaking, visual representations don't have to be visual. Audio techniques, such as spoken voice output, can be used, as can tactile feedback, such as found in forced-feedback joysticks.

The aesthetic aspects of the interface include the use of color, typography, line widths and styles, layout, and other stylistic aspects. These aspects can have a significant effect on user acceptance and comfort with the interface.

It is important that the interface be designed with a holistic approach. The visual elements must fit together. To illustrate this, examine Figure 2.10. What are the two objects? How are they constructed from their parts?

Now turn the book over to see the faces right-side-up. The pictures are composed of the same elements, but the relationship of the parts is as the user expects in one face and not in the other. This becomes obvious when the image is viewed in the proper context. Designers can fall into the trap of designing the interface in pieces that look fine on their own, but do not fit together when assembled. It is important to view the complete interface in context, as the user will.

In designing the operational aspects of visuals, the designer should be concerned with how well the visual conveys the purpose of the object being represented. In designing the aesthetic aspects, the designer should be concerned with providing a pleasing experience.

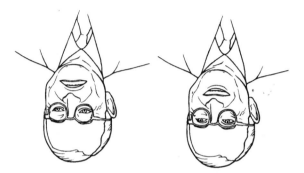

FIGURE 2.10   *Beside the fact that it is upside-down, what is wrong with this picture?*

2.8 Interaction Techniques

The designer's model specifies techniques to support user interaction with objects. A typical model includes more than one technique for each user interaction so that users can choose the technique that best suits the situation, their level of skill, and preferred style of interaction.

The designer's model should specify a pattern of interaction in which users interact with similar objects in similar ways and in ways that seem natural to users. Consistency should be a designer's goal for these aspects. Software development kits typically include multiple *controls*—such as buttons, menus, check boxes, and lists— to facilitate standardized interaction throughout the interface.

Written style guides typically provide substantial guidance for use of controls and the design of other interaction techniques. By using supplied controls and following rec-ommendations in a style guide, designers can avoid having to develop a complete model of interaction themselves.

2.9 Creating an Object Model

In user interface design, an object model describes objects and their properties, behaviors, and relationships with other objects as perceived by users in accomplish-ing a set of tasks. When creating an object model, the initial focus should be on the essential elements of use, clearly identifying functional purpose and boundaries of responsibility between objects.

It is also wise to keep in mind that not all users desire the same level of understanding. Some users will be perfectly content to learn the basics of operation and achieve an immediate degree of usefulness. Others will seek to become astute in the optimum use and control of the system, even to the degree of helping others troubleshoot and find problems.

The directed graph is a convenient form for creating an object model. The nodes of the graph can represent objects, while the arcs represent relationships such as "is a," "contains," and "uses."

Note

A directed graph consists of nodes and arcs. The nodes are typically shown as circles, rectangles, or bubbles, each of which represents an object. Text inside each node identifies the object. Arcs are lines drawn between nodes to identify relationships between the objects. Figure 2.4 is an example of a directed graph.

The object model approach is used to document the designer's model. The OVID methodology and this book provide you with the information you need to create a designer's model and ensure that it is accurately and completely conveyed to the implementors.

2.10 Developing a Designer's Model: The Automobile Example

In this section we explore the basic elements of a designer's model, the concepts surrounding it, and the benefits of creating and using one. To explore these issues, we will create a designer's model of something most of us are familiar with—the automobile. Before we start, let's quickly review the role of a designer's model and what we expect to get out of it.

We often refer to the aspects of UI design that deal with conceptual elements as *user interface architecture*. More specifically, UI architecture identifies the task-based *essential elements of use* and separates them from *mechanisms*. Another way to think about UI as architecture is to think about the separation of *semantics*, which is *what* the user is doing, from *syntax*, which is *how* the user is doing it. The goal of a UI architecture is to clearly identify functional intent and boundaries of responsibility. The designer's model is our vehicle for identifying, separating, and analyzing these crucial aspects.

Note

Essential elements of use are the conceptual elements of a system that allow the user to interact with a system. For example, steering, acceleration, and braking are essential elements of the interface to an automobile. Mechanisms are specific implementations of essential elements. A steering wheel is a mechanism for steering. Early automobile designers experimented with a variety of steering mechanisms, including tillers like those used in boats.

It also allows us to separate and focus on two dimensions of analysis: the designer's dimension (our own) and the user's dimension. The designer's dimension consists of defining a designer's model that provides the capabilities the users seek, while at the same time allowing implementors to choose various mechanisms and technologies to best match cost, scale, availability, and worker skill goals. Designs that embody this characteristic typically demonstrate superior flexibility, extensibility, and longevity.

The user dimension provides an assessment of users' understanding of the designer's model. As mentioned previously, for any individual user this can be measured by how closely his or her user's conceptual model (how they *think* the system works) matches the designer's model (how it actually *does* work).

We have found it useful to position users on an imaginary spectrum ranging from *naive* at one end to *astute* at the other. If we have an understanding and appreciation of the differing needs of these two extremes, we can better plan and design the facilities of a system. For example, for the naive user we might focus on ease of learning and immediate productivity, allowing him or her to accomplish meaningful tasks with a minimum of learning. For the astute user we think in terms of providing facilities that allow him or her to optimize usage and control, the ability to perform maintenance tasks, and possibly even do troubleshooting and develop workaround solutions.

With this background we are now ready to begin discovering the designer's model of the automobile. It really is *discovery,* not creation, in this case, because automobiles already exist. So in a way we are cheating, but since most people have probably never thought about the designer's model of an automobile, it provides a useful exercise with a very obvious ability to check our answers.

2.10.1 A Process for Defining a Designer's Model

In this section we introduce a simple process, which is elaborated on in the methodology in subsequent chapters. The process consists of the following steps:

1. Describe a scenario of use. For the automobile we might ask users "What does it do?" and "How do I use it?" For example, take the simple task of going somewhere. You get in the car, start the engine, put it in gear, release the parking brake, press the accelerator to speed up and let up to slow down, steer to change your direction, and press on the brakes to slow and stop.

2. From the task scenario, the designer identifies essential elements and roles. Highlight the nouns. Describe what they do and note any obvious aspects, such as the following, that might be used at the next level of detail:

- Engine—provides power to move the car (the engine requires energy)
- Transmission—couples the engine to the wheels (for speed and forward/backward direction control)
- Brakes—provide speed control (slow and stop only)
- Accelerator—provides speed control (speed up and slow down)
- Steering—provides direction control (left and right only)

3. Specify the relationships. In writing the descriptions of the relationships, we note that the engine provides speed to the wheels through the transmission, which adjusts or reverses the speed to the wheels. The brakes slow the speed of the wheels. The accelerator controls the speed of the engine. The steering controls the direction of the wheels and hence the direction of the car.

Thus far we haven't described how the engine produces the power to move the car, but we have noted that it requires energy. At this level of design our model describes cars powered by internal combustion engines burning gasoline and electric motors using batteries equally well. An illustration of this model is shown in Figure 2.11.

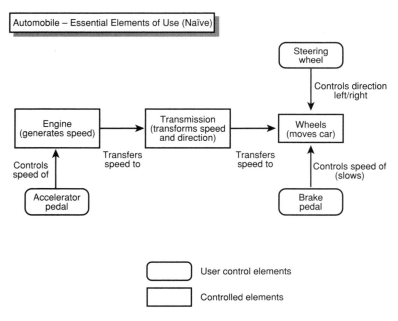

FIGURE 2.11 *A simple designer's model of the automobile.*

At this level of definition, several aspects of the design remain variable, providing the implementors with opportunities for choices. For example, the engine might be four, six, or eight cylinders. It may or may not use an overhead cam. The number of valves per cylinder isn't specified, nor is the fuel control system specified as a carburetor or fuel injection. It could even be an electric motor!

The transmission might be manual or automatic; it could be three, four, or five speeds; and it might have overdrive or might not. The car might use front-wheel drive, rear-wheel drive, or four-wheel drive, and the diameter of the wheels might be 13, 14, 15, or 16 inches.

What *is* fairly consistent at this level of definition are the essential elements of use and the user controls: accelerator, steering, and brakes. Although the implementors might choose from a large range of options for the engine, transmission, brakes, and steering, the elements of user control have become highly standardized worldwide. These standards enable us to rent a car and drive anywhere in the world, even if on a different side of the road than we are accustomed to. The use of standard controls allows us to concentrate on the task of driving.

Figure 2.11 is a model that depicts the knowledge of someone with a very basic understanding of automobile operation. Different people have different levels of understanding; hence, their models may vary in detail. Figure 2.12 depicts a model that includes more detail. The additional details still relate to *usage* aspects, and we continue to avoid any implementation-specific details.

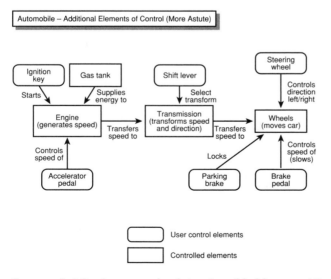

FIGURE 2.12 *A more complete designer's model of the automobile.*

Figure 2.13(a–d) demonstrates the wide variety of models that typically result when several people are asked to draw the model. These models were drawn by experienced user interface designers who had some knowledge of notation schemes, although each used a different notation. The variation in detail across the four models reflects the automobile users' perceptions of what is important.

The incompleteness evidenced in Figure 2.13(a) is typical. Interviewing users or having them answer questionnaires is sometimes necessary to prompt them to think about all the usage-oriented aspects. Talking through scenarios of use is often the most effective way to ensure that the model is relatively complete. Even if the model is not complete initially, it should become more complete as the iterative process of design progresses.

To be useful, a methodology must help us design new systems for which we have no current conceptual models. Completeness tests that do not depend on prior knowledge of the task domain are an important aspect of any robust methodology.

2.11 Summary

The following chapters will take you much deeper into each aspect necessary to understanding and building complete, durable, and extensible models. They introduce the notation and tools that make this methodology highly effective for communicating the intended design to an entire team.

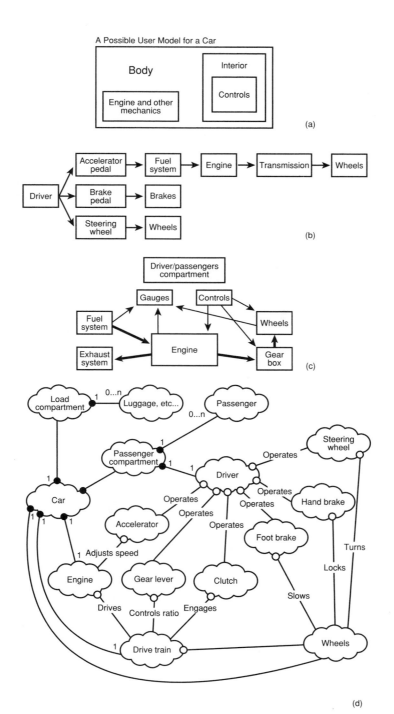

FIGURE 2.13 *Models of the automobile drawn by drivers.*

CHAPTER **3**

Object-Oriented User Interface Development

- **The software development life cycle**
  The software development life cycle involves planning, requirements analysis, modeling, design, prototyping, evaluation, and implementation. The phases of the life cycle are iterated upon until a successful design is created.

- **The development team**
  Object-oriented user interfaces are usually designed by teams because the work involved exceeds the time and talents of a single individual. Team members typically include a user interface designer, a usability specialist, a visual designer, and a software engineer.

This chapter places OVID within the software development life cycle and introduces the phases of the OVID methodology.

3.1 The Software Development Life Cycle

For many years, software development followed a sequential process called the *waterfall life-cycle model.* The number and names of the phases varied from one organization or project to the next, but they shared common characteristics of no overlap or iteration between phases. As each phase met its exit criteria, the output from that phase would pass on to the next phase and not be revisited. This model assumed that requirements do not change during the development cycle of the project. (See Figure 3.1.)

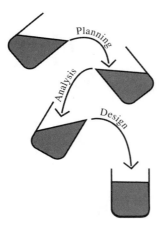

FIGURE 3.1 *The waterfall life-cycle model of software development.*

Today, it is generally recognized that the waterfall model is flawed. Requirements do change during the development cycle, and the design should change in response to those requirements. Problems encountered in any phase of the development process may require changes to the products of earlier phases.

The software development life-cycle approach has evolved from the waterfall model to a structured approach (Yourdon 1989). Barry Boehm (1988) describes a "spiral process," which addresses the deficiencies of the waterfall model. As problems are found, the process moves back to earlier phases and changes propagate through the process. (See Figure 3.2.)

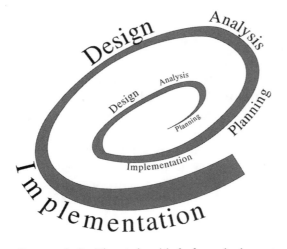

FIGURE 3.2 *The spiral model of software development.*

Iteration is very important in user interface design. It is extremely difficult to understand your users sufficiently and imagine a user interface so clearly that there won't be any surprises when users see it for the first time. Meeting your surprises throughout the design process is better than saving them for the end! By iterating design, implementation, and testing, you can fix user interface design problems along the way rather than doing expensive rework at the end of a project or shipping a product with user interface problems.

Do not view iteration as moving backward. Prototypes should be generated early in the process and updated as you go along. Prototypes provide a visible demonstration of progress throughout the project. Prototypes representing a stable implementation of portions of the planned program function can be delivered to users during development. This process is called *evolutionary development.*

Each phase of the spiral development process mirrors the activities of the entire project on a smaller scale.

The spiral process is typically used for object-oriented design, but object-oriented design has some specific activities unique to it. Dave Collins (1995) groups these activities into three clusters: finding the right conceptual model, making the objects in this model tangible to the users, and evaluating the result.

The conceptual models are determined through understanding the users and their tasks. The model is represented as objects, actions, and relationships. The second cluster of activities makes the conceptual model tangible by designing how the objects are represented and how the user interacts with them. The third cluster of activities involves evaluating the results of the first two clusters.

This spiral process is consistent with the OVID design process of determining the users' models, translating these into a designer's model, evaluating through prototypes and usability tests, and implementing the design.

3.2 Development Process Activities

The activities in the OVID OOUI development process are summarized here and are covered in detail in later chapters.

3.2.1 Requirements Analysis

OVID begins by understanding the users of the interface and the work they do. This understanding is not only important for the user interface, but it is helpful in the design of the whole system. Most object-oriented software engineering methodologies advocate a form of customer requirements collection for code design. This same information can be used for user interface design as well.

The umbrella term for the collection of information on user tasks is *task analysis*. In OO methodologies, task analysis is also known by terms such as *use cases* (Jacobson 1992; Booch 1994), *scenarios* (Wirfs-Brock et al. 1990; Rumbaugh 1991), and *scripts* (Rubin and Goldberg 1992).

3.2.2 Modeling

The modeling phase uses task information from the requirements phase to develop designers' models. These models identify the objects, interactions, and relationships between the objects, as well as the views in which the user will see the objects. These models are represented by class diagrams.

3.2.3 Design

The design phase instantiates the models as user interface elements, such as windows, icons, and interaction techniques. The design progresses from models to abstract visual design to concrete visuals.

3.2.4 Prototyping

Prototypes represent the interface design in forms that users and all members of the development team can understand. Prototypes range in fidelity from simple paper-and-pencil sketches to elaborate interactive programs. They serve as a common communication medium among all members of the team. They are vehicles for conducting user testing, starting at early stages of the design cycle.

3.2.5 Evaluation

Evaluation verifies that user requirements have been accurately understood and that the product being developed meets those requirements. Users are tested operating the prototype throughout the development cycle. This allows problems to be identified and appropriate design changes to be made as early in the design cycle as possible, when these changes are most easily made.

3.2.6 Implementation

OVID uses procedures and notation similar to those used in OO code development methodologies and some of the same tools as well. This allows the output of the interface design process to flow smoothly into code development.

3.3 The Development Team

The primary determinant of the success of a project is the quality of the people on the development team (Boehm 1981). A project may seem to fail due to any number of external factors, but these often turn out to be secondary effects. Good people manage the forces outside the team, pick the right tools, and develop good software. (See Figure 3.3.)

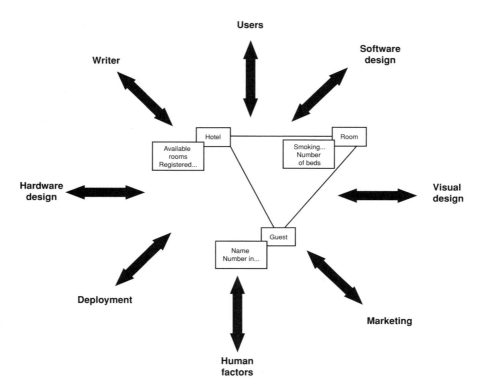

FIGURE 3.3   *Team development.*

OOUIs are usually designed by teams because the work involved exceeds the time and talents of a single individual (Collins 1995). We will describe some of the skills typically required on a successful software development team later in this chapter. Some members of the team may fill more than one role. Ideally, all members of the team know the other roles because the work needs to be coordinated across people with different skills and because some problems overlap multiple skill areas.

Communication between team members is vital to the success of any project. Figures 3.4 through 3.9 show the design of a tree swing from the viewpoint of various members of a development team. This is a joke that has circulated through many companies. The fact that it is so widespread shows how pervasive the problems of team development are.

FIGURE 3.4 *What the user needed.*

FIGURE 3.5 *As proposed by the project sponsor.*

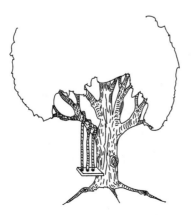

FIGURE 3.6 *As specified in the project request.*

FIGURE 3.7   *As designed by the systems analyst.*

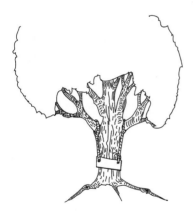

FIGURE 3.8   *As produced by the programmers.*

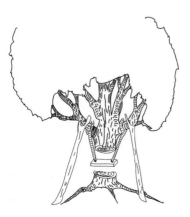

FIGURE 3.9   *As installed at the user's site.*

OVID helps to coordinate the efforts of a team. The models and prototypes developed in OVID provide ongoing documentation for the design to which all team members can refer. OVID specifies the key design tasks, and the project manager can use this information to allocate work to particular team members who are best qualified to perform each task.

The size and makeup of the development team depends on your company and the needs of the project, but a few of the common skills are summarized in the following sections.

3.3.1 Application Domain Expertise

Knowledge of the domain for which a system or application is being developed is critical if the system is to meet users' needs successfully. This knowledge is most important in the early stages of development, when the product is being defined, but it is also useful on a continuing basis as the design evolves and is evaluated.

Members of the development team may capture domain knowledge through interviews, task analysis, observation, training courses, and by working temporarily in the application domain. The best method, however, is to involve an end user or a small group of end users in the design process. They can provide the other members of the team with information on user requirements and act as user advocates. In designing a hotel application, for example, a desk clerk could describe current processes, define problems to be solved, answer questions, and evaluate proposed designs. These domain experts do not design the interface (because that requires specialized skills), but they provide the information necessary for the team to design an interface that meets users' needs.

3.3.2 The User Interface Designer

The UI designer balances customer needs and programming constraints to design an interface that meets the project goals. The UI designer constructs the models, identifies the objects and views, decides on the interaction techniques, and instantiates this with a concrete interface design. The UI designer receives much help and input from other team members, but is generally the focal point for all interface design activities.

3.3.3 The Usability Specialist

The usability specialist (often called a human factors engineer) is responsible for the efficiency and satisfaction characteristics of the user interface. The usability specialist is an expert in the interfaces between people and machines. He or she has a knowledge of the extensive body of research in human–computer interaction (HCI) and can use this information to provide advice on good design practice. The usability specialist typically performs the task analysis and other user requirements collection. He or she is also responsible for usability testing throughout the design process.

3.3.4 The Visual Designer

The visual designer creates the interface visuals. The visuals should be easy for the user to understand, efficient to read and use, and aesthetically appealing. This job is gradually changing to media designer as interfaces become richer in sound and other data types.

3.3.5 The Software Engineer

The software engineer or programmer is responsible for implementing the design, but should be involved in the design team long before implementation begins. The programmer can make the team aware of implementation constraints so that it can avoid expending effort on design paths that are not feasible. The programmer often develops prototypes so that team members and representative users can evaluate design alternatives or collect data from user testing.

PART II

Methodology

CHAPTER 4

Requirements and Analysis

- **Requirements gathering**
  Requirements gathering is the process of finding out what a customer requires from a software system.

- **Functional requirements**
  Functional requirements refer to both what the system does and what the user does.

- **User requirements**
  The objectives of the user requirements process are to identify who the users of the system will be, to understand the characteristics of these users, and to determine the usability requirements for the system.

- **Task analysis techniques**
  Task analysis techniques elicit descriptions of what people do and represent these in some form that is useful in the design of software systems.

OVID is a user-centered design (UCD) process. An interface should fit the needs, preferences, skills, and task requirements of the people who use it.

In UCD, users are involved in nearly all stages of development. In brief, the process is

1. Identify the users and their requirements

2. Identify and understand the tasks the users perform

3. Construct a user model

4. Conduct analysis, design, prototyping, and usability testing with continual user involvement

This chapter discusses how to determine user requirements.

User requirements are determined through a process called *task analysis*. This ensures that the user interface is designed to support the users' work activities.

Output of the task analysis is analyzed to identify objects and their relationships. This information is used to construct user and designer models.

4.1 Requirements Gathering

Requirements gathering is the process of finding out what a customer requires from a software system. A variety of techniques can be used to determine these requirements. Some common techniques include interviews, observation, tests of prior versions of the system, and system analysis.

You need to identify your users. In many cases, the audience covers a wider spectrum than anticipated. You should collect data on relevant end user attributes, such as education level, reading level, computer experience, and job classification.

Requirements gathering is concerned not only with determining needs, but with understanding them. This gives the designer the knowledge to set requirements for the system and also provides information to perform analysis as decisions come up during the development process. The result of requirements gathering is a representation of the problems with the current system and the requirements for a new system.

There are two categories of system requirements. *Functional requirements* specify what the system must do. *User requirements* specify the acceptable level of user performance and satisfaction with the system. These requirements are discussed in the following sections.

4.1.1 Functional Requirements

Developers should concern themselves with the whole human–computer system. Functional requirements refer to both what the system does and what the user does. *Task allocation* is the decision process through which activities are allocated to the computer and to the user. This step is deferred until after a task analysis has been done.

Functional requirements may be documented in a *functional specification*. The degree of formality for the functional specification varies greatly. Larger projects typically produce more formal and detailed specifications. The specification is often written in multiple levels, starting with abstract requirements (e.g., "the hotel management system should provide the capability to manage the allocation of rooms") down to very detailed requirements (e.g., "a confirmation dialog box must be provided to verify requests to delete a reservation").

Functional requirements are often constrained—for example, the client for the hotel reservation system may specify that the existing hardware and operating system be used for running the new software, placing limits on the type of interface that can be designed.

Functional requirements may be documented as a text document or as a data-flow diagram. (See Figure 4.1.)

FIGURE 4.1   *A data-flow diagram for a hotel registration function*

4.1.2 User Requirements

The objectives of the user requirements process are to identify who the users of the system will be, to understand the characteristics of these users, and to determine the usability requirements for the system.

Identifying the end users and their characteristics makes designers aware of whom they are designing for. This sounds obvious, but is all too often overlooked. In the absence of knowledge about end users, designers often design for people like themselves. This is seldom desirable because users typically differ from designers in their skills, task requirements, mental models, and preferences.

Usability requirements specify design objectives. The design can be evaluated against these objectives throughout the development process. Without explicitly specifying usability objectives, it is unlikely that these performance levels will be met. Through iterative design, usability measurements are compared against the goals and the design is refined. Explicit requirements help designers to concentrate their efforts in areas where usability is most critical.

User Classes

Many software systems are used by more than one class of user. A *user class* is a subset of the user population, which is similar in system usage and relevant personal characteristics. The members of a user class should be similar in their pattern of usage and usability requirements.

A given task may be performed by more than one class of user. For example, booking a room in a hotel reservation system may be performed by a desk clerk, a supervisor, or a trainee. User requirements should be developed for each distinct user class.

User class descriptions include information such as user's experience level, computer skills, use of other systems, education, motivation, and tasks performed.

The user classes should include not only direct users of the system, but also indirect users and remote users. *Direct users* are those who actually operate the system. A desk clerk is a direct user of a hotel management system. He or she will have operational requirements for the system. Indirect users are those who ask others to operate the system for them and make use of the output. The hotel manager may be an indirect user of the hotel management system. The manager may require that the system provide particular information, but not care how the information is generated. Remote users are those who depend on the input or output of the system. A guest is another indirect user of the hotel management system. For example, a guest does not use the system directly, but may require that statements be correct and complete.

Usability Requirements

Ben Schneiderman (1992) recommends the following five types of usability requirements:

- Time to learn
- Speed of performance
- Rate of errors by users
- Retention over time
- Subjective satisfaction

There are frequently tradeoffs among usability requirements. The relative priority of each requirement should be stated at the beginning of a project to aid in making these tradeoffs.

Each usability requirement should have a reason documented. We may, for example, require that training time for the hotel management system be less than two hours per employee because there is 50% annual turnover at the hotel, and a system that requires more extensive training would not be cost effective.

Specific criteria and methods of measurement should be specified for each usability requirement. These may be specified as targets, minimum acceptable levels, and/or acceptable ranges. The measures are referred to as *usability metrics* and are detailed in a *usability specification,* which are usually set up as tables. Examples of usability metrics include completion time for specified tasks, number of errors per task, and time to complete each task. (See Table 4.1.)

TABLE 4.1 SAMPLE ROWS FROM A USABILITY SPECIFICATION.

Attribute	Measuring Method	Worst Case	Planned Level	Best Case	Current Level
Installability	Time to install	1 hour	30 minutes	10 minutes	Many can't install
Configuration	Success rate	0%	90%	100%	80%
Editing	Satisfaction	1	6	7	5

Adapted from Whiteside et al. 1988

Usability requirements are established through interviews with existing or prospective users, business needs, and system analysis. Economic analyses are frequently done to determine whether development of a system meeting specifications will result in a net cost savings through increased efficiency, sales, better decision making, and so forth.

A number of techniques have been developed for collecting and documenting user requirements. The Human Factors in Information Technology (HUFIT) toolkit (Catterall et al. 1991) is designed to provide human factors input into the design of information systems. HUFIT consists of a number of tool sets. The planning, analysis, and specification (PAS) is designed to collect information about users' tasks and environments. The result of this analysis is a summary of user requirements and a functionality matrix. Data are initially gathered from all stakeholders in a project about the jobs they are intended to do and the costs and benefits associated with the project. User, task, and environmental characteristics are then identified and described in the functionality matrix, which forms the basis of informed task allocation and evaluation. Tradeoffs are recorded in the cells of the matrix. (See Table 4.2 and Figure 4.2.)

TABLE 4.2 AN EXAMPLE OF A LINE FROM A PAS TABLE.

User Groups	Task Goals	Benefits	Costs
Desk clerks	Check available rooms	Faster access to availability information	Time to learn new system
Manager	Determine occupancy level	Better inventory control	Time to generate report

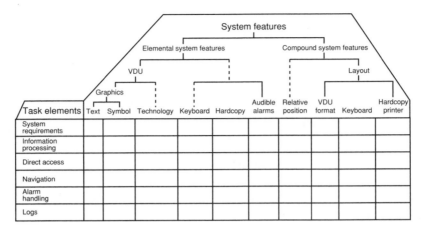

FIGURE 4.2 *An example of the HUFIT functionality matrix.*

4.1.3 Task Analysis Techniques

A wide variety of techniques are available for performing task analysis. These techniques all elicit descriptions of what people do and represent these in some form useful in the design of software systems. Although these techniques differ in their implementations, all the major techniques produce output that OVID can use. We will describe two techniques—hierarchical task analysis (HTA) and use case analysis—but you should feel free to choose an alternate technique if you are more familiar with it or it is more appropriate for your project.

Task analysis has the following goals:

- To understand what the user is trying to achieve (goals)

- To understand what the user does (task procedures)

- To understand the environment in which the user works (task context)

- To produce task descriptions

- To create an abstract interaction design that focuses on how the user will perform the tasks using the objects in the system, but without details of the UI design

- To produce task scenarios that will be useful in design, prototyping, and evaluation

Tasks are similar to the concept of function, but it is important to make a distinction. *Functions* are activities, processes, or actions that are available in a program. *Tasks* are the sets of actions performed by a user. In a hotel management system, one function is to maintain a table of room status (available, occupied, undergoing maintenance), and a related task is for the desk clerk to check room availability.

Tasks are groups of actions that together represent a meaningful operation. Pressing a key on the keyboard or moving the mouse does not constitute a task, but these are actions the user may perform in completing a task.

The various task analysis techniques differ in their use of terminology. For example, *goal* and *task* are used as synonyms in some techniques, but are defined quite differently in other techniques. For consistency, we have adopted the terms and definitions of Preece et al. (1994):

- A *goal* is the state of a system a person wishes to achieve (for example, a goal of a desk clerk may be to check in a customer).

- A *task* is the set of activities required, used, or believed to be necessary to achieve a goal. The goal of checking a customer in to a room requires several tasks, such as checking room availability, checking for a reservation, and entering the customer's billing information.

- An *action* is an operation the user performs in order to complete a task. The task of entering the customer's billing information will require a sequence of actions, such as pressing keys on the keyboard, moving and clicking the mouse, and requesting information from the customer.

- A *method* is a number of tasks or actions linked in a sequence (for example, providing keyboard-only or combined keyboard and mouse methods for performing the task of entering a customer's billing information).

- An *object* is the focus of an action. In entering a customer's billing information, the customer and the data are objects.

Hierarchical Task Analysis

Hierarchical task analysis (HTA) is one of the best-known forms of task analysis and has been in use for over 20 years. It begins with the collection of task scenarios and then creates graphical representations of high-level tasks, broken into constituent subtasks and actions. HTA iteratively identifies tasks, categorizes them, and breaks them into subtasks. In each pass, the accuracy of the decomposition is verified.

Information about tasks is collected from a variety of sources, including conversations with users, observation of users working, job descriptions, and operating manuals. A goal is listed as the desired state of the system and tasks describe the manner in which the goal may be achieved. Shepard (1989) provides a complete description of HTA.

A task scenario is an example of a task. It is a concrete instance with specific input and subtasks. A task scenario can be thought of as a test case. The task scenarios are documented as text descriptions. It is important to indicate who is performing each action (user, customer, system, etc.). The scenario looks much like a script for a scene in a play or movie. Figure 4.3 shows an example of a task scenario for a hotel management system.

Customer Check-in Scenario

Customer: "I would like to check in. I have a reservation under the name Smith."

Desk clerk: "Let's see." Searches reservation list for the name Smith.

System: Finds the reservation and returns customer information. Assigns a room and creates a key card.

Desk clerk: "Here is your key card, Mr. Smith. Your room is number 101."

FIGURE 4.3 *An example of task scenario notation.*

In designing a system, particular attention should be given to the most important tasks. The most important tasks are those that are frequent, time critical, or where errors are significant.

It is also helpful to create task scenarios for unusual circumstances. For example, ask end users "What is the most unusual request you have had in your job?" The system should not be designed specifically for these rare tasks, but should be flexible enough to accommodate them.

Express the task scenarios in terms of objects (nouns) and actions (verbs). This information will be important in later analysis.

In each scenario, ask if there is a simpler, shorter, or more natural way to perform the task.

Task scenarios are written for the way tasks are currently done and the way users would like to be able to perform the tasks. Designers may need to propose new task scenarios because the users may not know what is feasible.

Structure chart notation is used to document the task flow. The specific task information from the task scenarios is abstracted into general descriptions of tasks. Descriptions should be brief and should be independent of the computer system and user interface. These descriptions should represent the ideal, rather than the way tasks are currently conducted. The sequencing of activities is shown by ordering them left to right or top to bottom in the chart. Activities that may be repeated a number of times (iteration) are indicated by a small asterisk in the box. When one of a number of activities may be chosen (selection), a small circle is included in the box. A line in a box indicates the absence of an action. Figure 4.4 shows a flowchart for the goal of checking a customer in to a hotel.

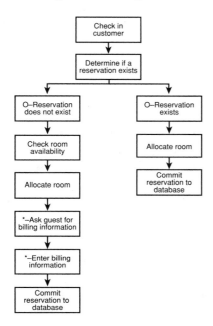

FIGURE 4.4   *An example of an HTA task analysis chart.*

Tasks can be broken into subtasks until no further granularity is possible or until you have reached the level of detail you desire. If you stop too soon, there is a risk of failing to identify some tasks. Continuing too far creates an overly complex task hierarchy and is not an effective use of time.

An HTA analysis can be described in three stages:

1. Starting the analysis

    • Specify the main task.

    • Break the main task into subtasks.

    • Draw out the subtasks, ensuring that they are logically and technically correct and that none are missing.

2. Progressing the analysis

    • Decide the level of detail required and the point at which to stop the decomposition. For example, we could decompose the hotel customer check-in task down to the individual keystrokes, to the field level (e.g., enter credit card number), or to the subtask level (e.g., enter all customer billing information).

- Decide whether to continue decomposing each task to the required depth (depth-first analysis) or to work on the next task (breadth-first analysis).

- The analysis continues until each task has been decomposed to the desired level.

3. Finalizing the analysis

- The analyses are checked and all decomposition diagrams generated.

- It is good practice to present the analysis to someone who was not involved in it, but who knows the tasks well to check for consistency.

This process produces task models representing the intended future structure of the tasks.

Use Case Analysis

Most object-oriented software design methodologies have adopted their own specific forms of task analysis. These analysis techniques include *use cases* (Jacobson 1992; Booch 1994), *scenarios* (Wirfs-Brock et al. 1990; Rumbaugh 1991), and *scripts* (Rubin and Goldberg 1992). All of these techniques provide user requirements suitable for use with OVID.

In this chapter we will describe the use case techniques because this is one of the most popular methods. For a more detailed description, see Jacobson (1992).

The use case defines the functionality the system should offer. It often serves as a contract between the developer and customer for the system, so it should be readable by nondesigners. The use case model defines the system from the user's perspective. The model uses actors to represent the roles the users can play and use cases to represent what the users should be able to do with the system. Each use case is a complete course of events in the system from the user's perspective.

Actors: Actors are used to model the prospective users. The actor represents a user type or category. When a user does something, he or she acts as an occurrence of this type. One person can instantiate (play the roles of) several different actors. Actors, thus, define roles that users can play. (See Figure 4.5.)

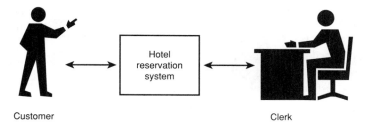

Customer   Clerk

FIGURE 4.5 *The customer and the clerk are actors in the hotel reservation system.*

The actors are used to model information exchange with the system. They can model users or other systems that communicate with the system being designed. Actors constitute anything external to the system being designed.

You can think of the actor as a class—that is, a description of behavior. The user can play several roles—that is, serve as many actors.

Actors who use the system directly are called primary actors—for example, the desk clerk is a primary actor in the hotel reservation system. Secondary actors exist so that the primary actors can use the system. The guest is a secondary actor in the hotel system. A guest does not use the system directly, but the clerk must collect information from the guest. There would be no need for the system at all if the hotel had no guests. Other systems may also be modeled as actors. For example, the hotel reservation system may request credit card account verification from another system as part of the check-in process.

Use Cases: A use case is a complete set of events specifying the interaction that takes place between an actor and the system. The collective set of use cases specifies all the existing ways of using the system.

Actors are useful for finding use cases. Each actor will perform a number of use cases in the system. By going through all actors and defining everything they will be able to do with the system, we will define the complete functionality of the system.

Use cases are constructed through interviews with users in which they are asked to describe the tasks they perform. The use case (Figure 4.6) is a text description of these tasks. Nouns in the use case are underscored as potential objects in the system, The most significant objects are underlined and bold.

> The **guest** makes a <u>reservation</u> with the **hotel**. The **hotel** will take as
> many <u>reservations</u> as it has **rooms** available. When a **guest** arrives, he
> or she is processed by the <u>registration</u> clerk. The <u>clerk</u> will check <u>the</u>
> <u>details</u> provided by the **guest** with <u>those that are already recorded</u>.
> Sometimes **guests** do not make a <u>reservation</u> before they arrive. Some
> **guests** want to stay in <u>nonsmoking rooms</u>.

FIGURE 4.6 *An example of a use case for a hotel management system.*

Use case scenarios should describe how the users will do their work when the new
system is in place—not how the work is done now or what the problems are with
how it is done now.

Use cases can be developed incrementally. You can focus on particular task areas,
create individual use cases for each area, and then later join them together to form
the complete requirements model. This helps to break the work into manageable
chunks and can also support parallel work by multiple analysts.

Weinschenk et al. (1997) recommend the following guidelines for creating effective
use case scenarios:

- *Write from the user's point of view, not the system's point of view.* In order to match
  the way the users should be doing their work, the scenario must be a list of
  user tasks. There is a tendency to start to describe what the system is going to
  do. If you really want a system description in your scenario, create a parallel
  scenario for the system.

- *Make sure you start with the user's tasks.* In order to be able to use the scenario to
  create a conceptual model and the interface design, you must have a listing of
  user tasks.

- *Include frequency information.* In order to create the most efficient interface
  design, you must document frequency of tasks in the scenario. If there are
  alternate paths, tasks, or decision points, you need to decide how frequently
  each path is to be taken. Will users be processing a new reservation most of
  the time or working with an existing reservation? This frequency information
  is critical if the scenario is to be most effective. What users do most should be
  easiest to do. Your design decisions and tradeoffs come in large measure from
  this frequency information—for example, if your scenario indicates that
  working with an existing reservation occurs 80% of the time, then during
  design you would start the screen flow for that task with a list of existing
  reservations. If, however, your scenario indicates that starting a new reservation occurs 80% of the time, you would start the screen flow for that task
  with a blank reservation ready to be filled in.

- *Make note of critical tasks.* Criticality must be balanced against frequency. The most important tasks are the ones to focus the most design attention on. A task may be important either because it is critical to the system or it is frequently performed.

- *Describe the future.* A scenario does not describe the user's tasks now, but the tasks a user will perform when the new system is in place. Documenting the current tasks may tend to lead you to a design that is not much improved from the current system.

CHAPTER 5

Constructing a Designer's Model

- **Finding objects**
  To begin developing an object-oriented user interface, it is first necessary to identify the objects needed. These objects include concrete objects, people, forms, and abstract objects.

- **Finding views**
  All user interaction is accomplished through views. When looking for views, it is important to examine the most frequent or important tasks.

- **Building state diagrams**
  State diagrams help determine how objects change states. A state diagram should be constructed for those objects where the actions allowed vary at different times.

In OVID, a key goal is to construct a designer's model that represents the application from the perspective of the user. There are four phases in this construction process:

1. Consider the objects that the user will deal with.

2. Suggest some views of these objects that will allow the user to interact with the objects needed to perform each task.

3. Document the details of how these interactions will occur in the form of new task descriptions.

4. Document the details of the specific interactions with individual views and with the related objects.

Although these parts of the process are spoken of as sequential phases, it is important to remember that OVID is an iterative process. No single phase will produce final results; all other phases must be executed. The cycle of these phases is shown in Figure 5.1.

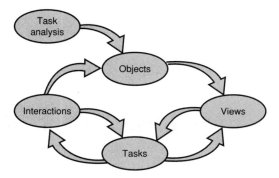

FIGURE 5.1   *The phases of OVID.*

In Figure 5.1, the arrows indicate the transfer of information between phases. Task analysis feeds first to object definition, but is also used when defining views, (new) tasks, and interactions. Note that transfer is both forward and backward in cases such as between view and task definition. When the system is complete, there should be a mapping between the newly defined tasks and the ones found during analysis.

5.1 Finding Objects

The initial information for constructing a designer's model comes from task analysis. Task analysis will reveal information about what the users do and which objects they work with. To start the development of your model, examine the text of the task analysis and mark the objects (nouns) in the text (for example, you can underline them). Figure 5.2 shows text that is part of a description of some tasks in a hotel; the objects are underlined and the most important objects are bold as well as underlined. This is the sort of information you should use to start your design.

This will probably produce a long list of objects, so your next task is to reduce this list to a manageable size. Include only key objects or the real core of the system. You will find five categories of objects useful:

- *Concrete objects*—those things that you can really touch

- *People who are the object of sentences*—the people who have things done for them, or to them, by the users of the system

- *Forms*—the documents that are used in the present system

- *People who are the subject of sentences*—the people who do things in the system
- *Abstract objects*—other things that you cannot touch or feel

> The **guest** makes a <u>reservation</u> with the **hotel**. The **hotel** will take as many **reservations** as it has **rooms** available. When a **guest** arrives, he or she is processed by the <u>registration clerk</u>. The <u>clerk</u> will check the <u>details</u> provided by the **guest** with those <u>that are already recorded</u>. Sometimes **guests** do not make a <u>reservation</u> before they arrive. Some <u>guests</u> want to stay in <u>nonsmoking rooms</u>.

FIGURE 5.2 *Typical task descriptions from task analysis.*

From now on you should look for or deal with the objects in the order of these categories. These categories will not have a fundamental effect on the result, but they will help you to find the more important things first. The key objects of your system will most likely be concrete objects or those people who are the objects of sentences. Start with these and, for each, ask yourself whether the system could still be called by the same name if that object were removed. For example, if you were building a hotel system, you could not continue to call it a hotel system if you took away the rooms. However, if you took away the guest registry, then you could still have a hotel system; you are merely finding another way to run the business. Figure 5.3 shows objects grouped into the five categories used to help with object priority. You should search from left to right when searching for objects to use in the solution.

Concrete Objects	People (Object)	Forms	People (Subject)	Abstract Objects
Hotel room	Guest	Reservation bill	Registration clerk Cleaner Manager	Guest–details

FIGURE 5.3 *Objects found in a hotel reservation system.*

In addition to using these groupings, you should use frequency of occurrence as a guide to important objects. Both those objects that occur in frequent tasks and those objects that occur in many different tasks should be given priority. When listing objects in the five groups, mark the ones that occur many times or the tasks that are performed often.

Next, for every object that you have listed, write a short, one-clause sentence that describes the object. The sentence should not contain any ifs, ands, or buts. This exercise of reducing an object description to a single sentence ensures that each object is kept as straightforward as possible so that it will be easier for a user to remember the object's role. The process also weeds out those objects where the definition cannot be agreed on. If you cannot agree, put the object on one side and come back to it on a later iteration.

A good goal for this phase of design is to produce a list of three to six objects that will be the core of the system. Once the list has been reduced to about this number, it is time to begin drawing the model. Each object is represented on the diagram by a rectangular shape. If you are using a tool such as Rational Rose to produce the diagrams, you should store the sentences that describe the objects in the description section of each object.

Note

Rational Rose is an object-oriented CASE (computer-aided software engineering) tool and is part of the tool suite developed by Rational Corporation. Another such tool is Together J from Object International Inc.

The next information to record is the relationships between the objects. Look at each task description and decide which relationships are formed during each task. One way to think about these relationships is that they answer the question "Why do I need an object of this class?" For example, when a guest first calls the hotel, he or she is making a plan to stay at the hotel, and the hotel needs to record information about everyone who has such a plan. On the class diagram, the relationship between the objects is shown as a line connecting those objects. The text describing the relationship is written near the line.

Figure 5.4 shows main hotel objects and their relationships. The line between hotel and guest represents the *plan to stay* relationship. In both cases the relationship allows any number of objects to participate. In this case, you can say that "any number of guests can have plans to stay at a hotel" and "a guest may plan to stay at any number of hotels." The line between guest and room represents an actual stay in the hotel; a specific room is assigned. Again, many guests and hotels can be involved. A *has a* relationship, shown with a diamond and an arrow, is used between hotel and room; this represents the permanent composition of the hotel. This is read as "the hotel has n rooms."

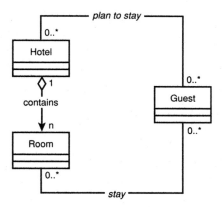

FIGURE 5.4 *Main hotel objects with relationships.*

It is also possible to record much more detail about the relationship. In the same way that a single sentence is constructed to describe an object, a similar sentence should be constructed and recorded to describe each relationship. In the diagram, you may also include a phrase that describes the relationship from the perspective of one of the objects. This will clarify the direction of the relationship when it is not obvious—it is called the *role*. A third piece of documentation for a relationship is its *cardinality*. Cardinality describes how many instances of the objects may enter into the relationship. For example, in the case of a hotel, it is possible to have no guests planning to stay and equally possible to have many guests planning to stay, so the cardinality of the relationship is formalized as 0 to $\star$(asterisk), which is written as $0..\star$. Note that the cardinality is written at the far end of the relationship line. In Figure 5.5 you should read "the hotel has *n* rooms" and "the guest stays in a room." In contrast to the guest's plans, once a hotel has been established, it is unlikely that the number of rooms in the building would change, so the number of rooms is fixed and shown as *n* in the diagram. It uses a *has a* relationship because this is considered a permanent condition. Also notice in Figure 5.5 that there are several relationships between hotel and room. Smoking is an attribute of the room that has been modeled externally.

Another sort of relationship that must be drawn is one that indicates where information needs to be gathered for a task. For example, we may need to know which rooms in the hotel are empty. To indicate this, a line is drawn between hotel and room and labeled *free*. This line represents the need for information about free rooms in the hotel.

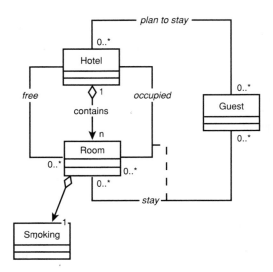

FIGURE 5.5 *A model of hotel objects showing more relationships.*

Note

Again, if you are using a recording tool, then you will find it easier to record all this detail in description sections associated with each relationship.

Having decided on a short list of objects and the relationships between them, it is now a good time to verify this with as many members of your team as possible. Getting strong agreement on the short list provides the best foundation for further work. You should also get some of your users to assess the list.

5.1.1 A More Detailed Model

You have your foundation, taken from the most significant task. Now it is time to include more of the objects that you found in the other tasks in the analysis information. But objects should only be introduced to the model when you have shown that there is a clear need for them in the system. In some cases this will mean that you will not introduce some objects until you've made several iterations on the model. Some will never appear in the solution.

OVID has a modeling rule that shows the need for some objects: Where the cardinality at *both ends* of a relationship contains *n* (e.g., *n*, 0..*, 1..*), a *many to many* relationship exists, and you must introduce an object, called an *association object*, to record details of the individual relationships. (For example, the relationship between the guest and the hotel, called *plan to stay*, is a *many to many* relationship.) So an object must be introduced to record each individual plan. Here, the object required can be called a *reservation*, picking up a name from one of the objects we had already listed from the task analysis. The new object is drawn near the relationship line and connected to that line with a dashed line. (See Figure 5.6.)

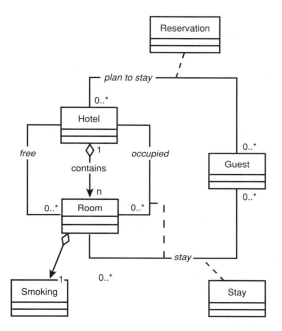

FIGURE 5.6 *The reservation is added to the hotel diagram.*

Frequently you will discover that the forms you found from the task analysis will be the perfect objects to represent these relationships. This is because the forms exist in the current system in order to record this sort of information. Scan your model for *many to many* relationships and add the required association objects to it.

It is important that during the modeling you attempt to record all questions or any other information that you discover. Some of the questions or comments will be easily associated with a single object or relationship—for example, if you are unsure about a relationship, then put a comment in the description of that relationship so that the information is not lost. In other cases you may need a further modeling technique to record your comments. You can use a dashed line between two relationships to indicate some further information about how two relationships may coexist—for example, in the case of a hotel, there is a relationship between a room being occupied and a guest staying in a room. When a guest is staying in a room, it is occupied. This information is shown in Figure 5.6 as a dashed line between the relationships. In Figure 5.6, the reservation object is used to model each instance of the *plan to stay* relationship between the hotel and the guest.

5.1.2 Alternate Models

It is often possible to model some objects in several ways. Remember, your model is attempting to record the way that users will think about the system. Try to look at the objects from many perspectives. Imagine yourself as one of the people working with the system. How would you think about the objects that you can see? Drawing the model from each perspective and showing only the objects and relationships that a particular user experiences can be a powerful tool. Most modeling tools allow you to create copies and subsets of diagrams in order to do this.

Sometimes these different perspectives will reveal apparent inconsistencies in the present implementation. Wherever there is an inconsistency, there is room for mis-communication and error. You should try to remove these by refactoring the objects. You can split objects into parts and then use these parts to create clusters or compositions that explain the varying perspectives. From the perspective of the check-in clerk, the hotel has many reservations and the guest may be considered an attribute of each reservation, but from the perspective of a travel agent, the guest may have a collection of reservations and the hotel is considered an attribute of each reservation. Figure 5.7 shows examples of alternate perspectives of a model. Part (a) shows the designer's model for the hotel, guest, and reservation. Part (b) shows the same objects from the perspective of the registration clerk, where the guest is treat-ed as a part of the reservation. Similarly, (c) shows the same objects from the per-spective of a travel agent or a guest using an online booking service.

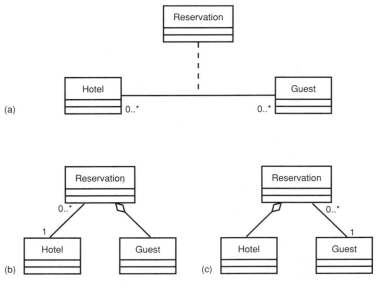

FIGURE 5.7 *Alternate perspectives of one model.*

In some instances, a subclass relationship may be useful. This relationship indicates that, even though two objects may really be very similar, some of the users of the system think of them as distinct types. In a hotel system, for example, guests who are currently staying at the hotel are dealt with differently than guests who are not currently resident. So it may be useful to model "staying guests" and "guests with reservations" as different classes of guest. Figure 5.8 shows how this can be drawn and how some of the relationships apply to each of these subclasses of guest. If you are able to draw several plausible models at this stage, you should ensure that these are validated in discussions or tests with your users.

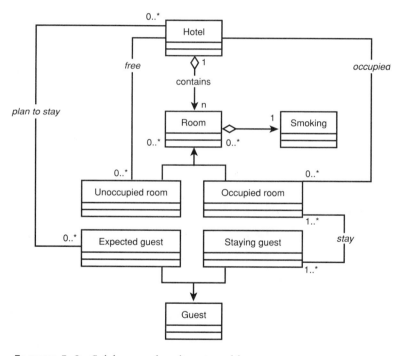

FIGURE 5.8 *Subclasses used as alternate models.*

5.1.3 Modeling Attributes

Attributes of objects, those things with a *has a* relationship, can be modeled in two different ways. The choice between these techniques depends on the significance of the attribute. There is no material difference between the models; it is merely a cosmetic convenience to avoid clutter in the diagrams.

You will note that in Figure 5.8 the smoking attribute of the room has been drawn as an attached object with a *has a* relationship. For any attribute that you think is significant, you should model it this way. However, if no further connections are made to the attribute during later stages, it can be written inside the box of its owning object to reduce clutter. Figure 5.9 shows such a diagram. Part (a) shows a form of modeling that may be used initially for any attributes or parts of other objects. If no relationships to the attached object are formed during later iterations, this can be redrawn as shown in (b), which shows the same information and is used when no relationships have been formed to the smoking attribute.

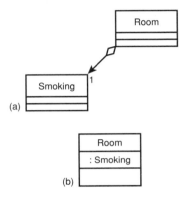

FIGURE 5.9 *Smoking modeled as an aggregated object and as an attribute.*

Users can only interact with objects using views of those objects. So once a detailed model of objects has been constructed, the next phase of design is to determine which views should be made available.

5.2 Finding Views

As with objects, you will find views by reference to the tasks that the user must perform. Again, when looking for views, you should examine the most frequent or important tasks first. You should look at the information that the user needs to read or supply in order to complete each task. You will see that this information is recorded in the designer's model as the relationships between objects and the attributes of objects. The information about each view is recorded in the model as another object. It is augmented with a note (shown as a box with a dog-eared corner) containing the task-related detail. This also helps to distinguish the views from the other objects.

Note

This technique for showing views is used because there is no formal notation for this concept in Unified Modeling Language (UML). Although the information is held in the notational representation for an object, it should not be thought of, either by the designer or the user, as an object.

The view-object and the note both serve a role in the model. The *view-object* is used in a later phase of design to record the state information about the view so that the cumulative effect of users' actions can be documented. The *note* records an abstract description of the items in the view and is mainly used in the design of the view during implementation. In our hotel example, the first view that has been added is one that enables a desk clerk to check in a guest when the guest arrives. In order to do this task, the clerk must have information about the plan to stay (or reservation) for that guest (if he or she has one) and also about the rooms in the hotel that are free, including some detail about each room. You will see in Figure 5.10 that a note has been added with dashed lines (called *note anchors* in Rose) drawn between the note and the relationships in the diagram. The dotted lines from the box indicate that the information from the plan to stay and the free relationships is needed to complete this task. In the early iterations of a design, it is not essential to write any other information in the note. The presence of the note and the lines connecting it to the associations of an object are sufficient. In later stages, or when specific attributes of an object are identified, you must insert this detail into the note.

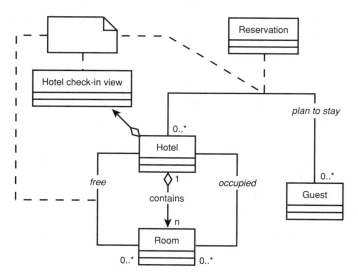

FIGURE 5.10   *The check-in view and its connection to the hotel.*

A view has been defined that is appropriate for a task, but which object is this a view of? Which of the objects should users think they are dealing with? Another OVID modeling rule comes into play here: The rule for attaching views is that a view must show only information that is available in the host object. This means that the host object for any view must be at the convergence of all the relationships that are needed to be shown in that view. So once you have determined which relationships are to be shown in a view for any task, you should connect the object representing the view to the object where all those relationships converge. For example, we find that the view used for check-in is associated with relationships that converge on the hotel. If there is no object in the system that can satisfy this rule, you should break the view into smaller component views that can satisfy this rule.

During the first iteration, you should normally leave the descriptions of the views at a fairly high level. On later iterations you will need to show more detail.

5.2.1 Combining Views

In any user interface system a view may be composed of several more specific views. For example, the hotel's views may combine views of rooms and guests. In the model, this is shown as further views, and those views are connected by associations. These views are not normally defined until you have a clear understanding of the exact details needed for each task and should not be confirmed until after some level of user testing.

As you proceed to examine each of the tasks in the task analysis, you may find that you are able to discover clusters of information that are used in many tasks. In some cases this means that you can simply reuse the views that you already have in order to perform these later tasks. In other cases you may decide to factor the common parts of a view into a partial view, which can be used for many tasks. You should show this reuse of views in the diagram by connecting the various objects that represent the views. By convention we employ the *uses* or *depends on* notation, which is diagrammed with a dotted line that ends in an arrow.

Figure 5.11 shows the hotel system with two views. The hotel check-in view *uses* or *depends on* the room view for check-in to complete the information that is needed for the task. Because the details about the room are all attributes, they must be shown in detail in the box attached to the room view for check-in. The relationship would contain documentation of exactly how the views should be combined. If views are combined, then there must be some relationship between the hosting objects (hotel and room in this case) that shows the reason for the combination. There must also be a dotted line to that relationship from the box of the main view.

Some of the views that you have defined need to display details of the associated objects. To do this, a view of the associated object must be defined. You should specify these views using exactly the same techniques you used in the other views you have found. Once the new view is available, you should connect it to the first view with a *uses* relationship.

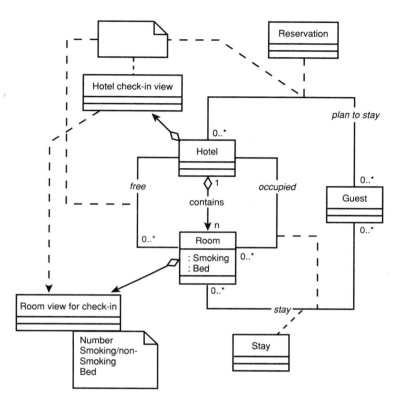

FIGURE 5.11 *Two related views used for check-in.*

In the *depends on* or *uses* relationship you must record the technique you will use to reach one view from the other. You could, for example, decide that the second view will be reached by a user action. This could be implemented as a navigation using a hypertext link, a pushbutton, or some other form of navigation command. Alternatively, you could decide to use some type of view composition, either embedding the second view in the first or combining the views in frames or on notebook pages. In this last case, you should be aware that you are giving the user a strong message that the second object is a property of the first. You should reexamine it to ensure that this is satisfactory. The relationship between the two objects should be reclassified as a *has a* connection. If there are other associations with the second, contained object, then you must decide if they are still needed. Properties or attributes are not allowed to have associations that are independent of their parent object.

Figure 5.12 shows some views of, from left to right, the hotel, room, and guest details that might appear once the guest has been checked in. Note that these views have been designed so that the room detail does not show from the hotel view—another window or pane is implied. However, the guest can be shown in place in the room view—the further detail being an enlargement—or in a window on its own.

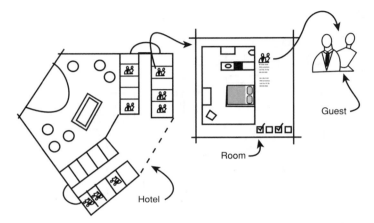

FIGURE 5.12 *Views connected by reference and composition.*

The next process involves describing in detail how tasks will be accomplished in the future and how the user interacts with the objects.

5.3 Creating a Detailed Task Description

All user interaction is accomplished through views. Whenever a user must deal with an object, the user must be presented with a view that is suitable for the tasks he or she wishes to perform. The next part of the OVID process involves adding objects to the system to represent the users of the system and showing how these users employ each of the views to perform their tasks. In early iterations it is sufficient to show only the interactions between users and views in most cases. However, in later iterations you should also show the details of the interactions between the views and the objects they represent.

As with all the processes within OVID, the work begins by referring to the task analysis with which we started. In this case we must create a task diagram, which represents each of the tasks or subtasks we will enable in the final system. Again, the frequency or importance of the task is used as a guide to help us tackle the tasks in an appropriate order. In an example of a hotel system, we have started with the check-in task.

Figure 5.13 shows in detail how the desk clerk would perform the task. The first column in the diagram represents the desk clerk. Each arrow in the diagram that goes from one column to another shows an interaction between these two items. (Arrows may also go to the column in which they started—this indicates an interaction within an object.) The first line of the diagram shows the clerk using a view in order to look for the reservation for that guest. At this stage, there is no detail of how the information in the view is employed. However, it is possible to write a much more detailed diagram on later iterations. This will involve a study of the state diagrams that have been produced in the fourth phase. This diagram assumes that the hotel check-in view is open before the task starts; this detail could also be added to the diagram. Words in parentheses after an interaction name are the names of items of information that are passed (or *parameters*, in programming terms).

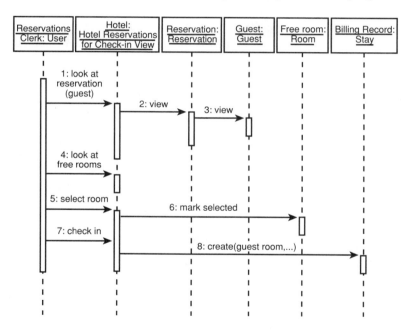

FIGURE 5.13 *An interaction diagram for the check-in task.*

Notice in Figure 5.13 that we have included details of how the views of objects interact with their host object. Also, the details of how objects interact with each other have been included. Remember that you do not need to supply all this information at first, but the more information you provide early in the process, the less likely you are to have misunderstandings later.

This task diagram of the hotel system is only one of many such diagrams. An important role of these diagrams is to collect a list of all interactions with each object. By examining each column of a diagram, you will find the names of all the arrows that end at that column. This list of arriving arrows is a list of the interactions that the object or view must support. You will use this list during the next phase of your design in order to produce details of how the object or view works. If you are using a tool such as Rational Rose to record your work, you will find that you are able to have the tool gather this information for you. Each of the interactions can be written as a method for that object. (Details of how to perform this can be found in the help information for Rational Rose.)

5.4 Building State Diagrams

Each object in the system can be described by a finite state machine. A *finite state machine* is a system where an object is always in one known state, and there is a fixed list of these states. In OVID we use a state diagram called a *Harel diagram* to show the states. In such a diagram each of the states is represented by a small rounded rectangle, and the name of the state is written in the rectangle. The diagram also shows how the object changes state. This is done by drawing an arrow from one state to another.

A state diagram should be constructed for those objects where the actions allowed vary at different times: They have a life cycle. In a hotel system, for example, a room must be occupied by only one guest (or party). A state diagram must be constructed for a room so that the user interface can enforce this rule. By knowing when it is valid to check a guest into a room, the views of the room can disable the mechanisms in order to prevent the user from performing the check-in task at times when it is not allowed. For some other objects, it is not necessary to produce a state diagram (for example, the states of a hotel are not important). All the actions that can be applied to the hotel can be applied at any time and in any state.

When you decide that a state diagram is needed, you should begin each diagram with a steady state of an object. For example, in the case of a hotel room, we will start with the room in the free state. Examine the task descriptions that were produced in the previous phase and look at the list of actions that affect the object in question. Consider what should happen when these actions are applied. Do this in the order in which the actions occur in the tasks. After the application of an action, what best describes the new state of the object? Draw an arrow from the steady state to a new state and label it with this new description. For example, Figure 5.14 shows the first two states found for the room. The room starts in the free state, and after the check-in action (or event), it will be in the occupied state.

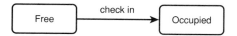

FIGURE 5.14 *The first two states found for a room, shown in a Harel diagram.*

Continue this process by applying all the actions you have documented in your task descriptions. Each time you produce a new state, you should consider how well it matches with all the previous states. You may have two very similar states that can really be treated as one. You should also consider when actions that were initially given different names are really the same action but performed at different times.

At the end of this process, you should have produced a state diagram that shows the life cycle of your object. (For example, Figure 5.15 shows the normal states of the room and the normal progression from state to state.) If there are a large number of states for an object (more than six), you should consider simplifying this object. The objects that have a large number of states (complex behavior) are difficult for users to understand and employ correctly in their tasks. Simplification may involve splitting an object into parts. Do this by looking for groups of states that have few interactions with other groups or even no connection. Split the object and try to describe it in terms of two objects that interact with one another. Remember that you must continue to apply the rules for objects, such as having a single-sentence description with only one clause.

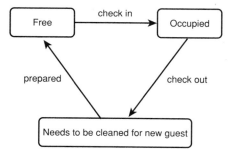

FIGURE 5.15 *A complete Harel diagram for a room.*

In producing the state diagram, you have considered the actions on an object in the normal sequence of occurrence. But the user interface must be able to cope with users who attempt to perform steps out of sequence. To make it easier to consider all these cases, a different form of documentation for the finite state machine is used. Rather than a Harel diagram showing rectangles and arrows, the information is transferred to a *state table*. In this table, each column represents a state of the object.

Each row represents one of the actions that may occur. The cell at the intersection of a row and column shows what happens for that event in that state.

The states and events can be transcribed from the state diagram to the state table. You will find that only a few of the cells in the table will contain information. For the hotel, the state table for a room is shown in Figure 5.16. The entries in this state table correspond to those in the Harel diagram shown in Figure 5.15. Empty cells are the state/action pairs that have not been considered in the design. Figure 5.16 shows how the cells of the table are used to contain documentation about the transitions from one state to another. Each cell can also contain any other details about the transition that you are able to determine. The amount of detail may vary from object to object.

	Free	Occupied	Needs to be cleaned for new guest
check in	Start stay record. Change to occupied.		
check out		Complete stay record. Change to needs to be cleaned for new guest.	
prepared			Change to free.

FIGURE 5.16 *The state table for a room.*

The empty cells in the table represent actions that have not been considered for some states. These actions are not on the normal path for any task. However, a user may attempt one of these actions at any moment. To complete the design, you must consider each of the actions and determine an appropriate response. This response will vary from one situation to another. Some actions will perform some useful functions in more cases than you initially thought. They are useful extensions to the system. Other actions will need to be blocked so that the user cannot send the system to an invalid state. A third, more trivial, case is that some actions are impossible to achieve in certain states.

In the example of the hotel room, let us consider one of the actions: check-in. When the room is free, it is perfectly normal to check in a guest. This transition has already been documented as part of the normal task flow. When a room is occupied, it is not valid to check another guest into that room. So, at the intersection of the occupied state (column), and the check-in action (row) we must document that this action is not allowed. When an action is not allowed, we should also consider which mechanisms will be used to signal this to the user. A nearly complete state table for the hotel room is shown in Figure 5.17, where all the state/action pairs have been considered. Those shown in gray boxes were the normal life cycle. The other five entries represent cases that have to be considered to have a complete design.

	Free	Occupied	Needs to be cleaned for new guest
check in	Start stay record. Change to occupied.	Not allowed.	?
check out	Can't happen, there is no guest.	Complete stay record. Change to needs to be cleaned for new guest.	Can't happen, there is no guest
prepared	Should not happen.	Should not happen.	Change to free.

FIGURE 5.17 *A state table for a room, complete in all cases except for checking guest into a room that needs to be cleaned.*

The cases where a mechanism can be disabled completely to prevent an action are relatively straightforward. There are more complicated cases where further design decisions must be taken in order to produce a satisfactory user interface. In the hotel example, there is a difficult decision to be made for the case where the check-in action occurs at the time when the room needs to be cleaned. If the hotel is almost full and a guest arrives early, you may wish to offer better service to the guest by allowing some form of check-in even when the room is not quite ready for use. This is ultimately a business decision, but the system must be written to account for either case.

If the decision is taken to allow check-in to a dirty room, the state diagram must be redrawn. A further state must be added to show that the room has a guest checked in but also still needs to be cleaned. The check-in action from the state needs to be cleaned will cause a transition to this new state. The designs recorded in other phases (class diagrams and task diagrams) will have to be updated as a result of this change.

Users may only cause actions to occur if a mechanism is provided in a view for that to happen. In OVID, we use the documentation associated with any action to record all the mechanisms that are available to the user to perform the action. If a state diagram is drawn using a tool such as Rational Rose, then the information can be recorded in the documentation for the state transition arrows. In a state table, this information is recorded in the cell where the transition or action name has been written. For example, in the case of check-out, we might write

> Check-out: Press the check-out button; drag the guest from the room; say "check out guest in room 104."

It is these mechanisms that must be disabled when an action is not allowed. So, when the program makes a transition to any state, the mechanisms for any actions that are not allowed must be disabled. For example, when the hotel room is changed to empty, the button for check-out should be disabled.

Design changes in any of the four phases of the OVID process can have effects on the other phases. No design is valid until it has proved to work effectively for the users.

CHAPTER 6

Converting the Designer's Model to an Implementation

- **Creating a programmer's model of the environment**
  You must decide in which environment, operating system, programming tools, and system services your product is to be used.

- **Decomposing the designer's model**
  You must produce a metamorphosis of the designer's model into the programmer's model. The objective is to show enough detail so that there is a direct mapping between elements in the two models.

- **Translating the elements of both models to an executable form**
  Examples show how models are used to create a UI design.

Developing the designer's model is at the core of OVID. However, it is not sufficient to develop a designer's model—the model must be converted to a programmer's model and then to an implementation that can be deployed before it will be of any benefit. This process of conversion has three parts:

1. Create a programmer's model of the environment into which the system will be placed.

2. Decompose the designer's model to a sufficient level of detail to match the programmer's model.

3. Translate the elements of both models to an executable form.

In this chapter, we will first describe these steps in more detail and then provide two examples to illustrate the process.

6.1 Creating a Programmer's Model of the Environment

You must first decide in which environment, operating system, programming tools, and system services your product is to be used. In some cases, you will be able to make these decisions for an individual system. In many more cases, the choice of environment will be made for you. The environment will be dictated either by the market into which the system is being sold or by the company for which it is being built. This may be Microsoft Foundation Classes (MFC), Borland Delphi, Lotus Notes, or any of a number of other implementation vehicles. Whichever it is, the steps are the same, but the level of detail in each step will vary.

One of the factors you might consider is the speed of implementation. A Notes implementation can be built very quickly. This normally avoids the need to build a separate prototype of the interface. The price for this is that you have less freedom in design. At the other end of the spectrum, you may be using C++ and MFC, where alternative prototypes are essential. More detail on these is discussed later in the book.

Several aspects of the environment must be modeled. Perhaps the most important one is the visual toolkit, or framework, you will use. You need to understand it and know how its elements relate to those in the designer's model. The best way to do this is to obtain or generate a programmer's model of the toolkit. You will not need to have one that shows all the internal subtleties of the toolkit itself. For example, you do not need to know exactly how each class is related to every other one. In order to do the decomposition of the designer's model, you will only need to know the main components of the library and how they can be used to represent the elements of the designer's model.

Our two examples were built with different technologies. The first is a Lotus Notes database, which implements part of the hotel system described in previous chapters. The second example is of a telephone called RealPhone, a Windows 95 application built using MFC, which allows your computer to act as a speakerphone.

6.2 Decomposing the Designer's Model

What you must produce is a metamorphosis of the designer's model into the programmer's model. Once you have both models, you must bring them to an equivalent level of detail. Because the environment model is normally at a much lower level of detail than the designer's model, this normally means that you need to further decompose the designer's model.

The objective is to show enough detail so that there is a direct mapping between elements in the two models. If your environment has a pushbutton to allow the user to trigger an action, then for each action that is required in a view, you should add another view to the designer's model that will map to the pushbutton.

During this process you will change the skills that you apply to the task: of user interface design at the start and programming at the end. By driving the process from the designer's model, you should be able to ensure that the integrity of the design remains until the end.

Besides decomposing views into visual elements from the toolkit, you must also decompose the objects to a level where they can be mapped to the environment. In some cases, this will be a simple mapping to some data store. In other cases, you will have to map to elements that are already well defined. The following two examples show these two cases: The hotel system has freedom to define a database that suits the implementation and the telephone has to cope with the existing telephone line.

6.3 Example 1: The Hotel System

For the purposes of this section, we will first think about a hotel system and consider an implementation being built using Lotus Notes. Notes is a high-level toolkit, which leads to a simple design process. Later, we will consider the development of a telephone using MFC, which requires a more detailed design process.

6.3.1 Modeling Lotus Notes

The main elements of a Notes implementation are databases, documents, scripts or agents, views, forms, and fields. Their relationships are shown in Figure 6.1, which is a summary of the architecture of Lotus Notes. We have not concerned ourselves with the role of Lotus Script and the Formula Language at the moment because these mainly provide the programming mechanisms or methods for the other elements. Note that the document field also has several subclasses, which can be roughly mapped to those of the field. However, these are normally dictated by the field that generates that document field. To create your own implementation, you will need to have a model of the environment you are using at a similar level of detail.

The documents, document fields, and document properties in Notes will be mapped to objects in the OVID designer's model. The views, forms, and fields will be mapped to views. A more complete version of the classes in the designer's model we developed in Chapter 5, "Constructing a Designer's Model," is shown in Figure 6.2, which shows all of the objects required for the check-in process and the views of these objects.

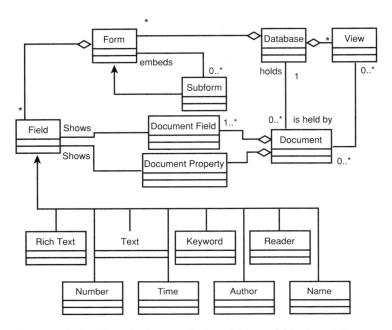

FIGURE 6.1   *The main elements of a Lotus Notes model implementation.*

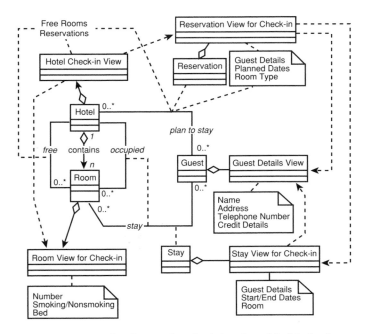

FIGURE 6.2   *A class diagram from the designer's model of the hotel system.*

The hotel is to be represented by a Notes database. Next, we map the remaining objects to documents. So room, guest, stay, and reservation will be documents in the implementation. The attributes of these objects will be mapped to document fields. For the moment, we will only concern ourselves with attributes of room, which are number, smoking, and bed. The number attribute maps readily to the number field type. The smoking and bed attributes map to the keyword field type. In addition to this, another field will be required to hold the state of the room, as prescribed by the state diagram.

The other elements shown in Figure 6.2 are the views that have been defined for check-in. The hotel check-in view is best implemented as a Notes view because it will need to show lists of two objects: rooms and reservations. The room view for check-in does not need to be implemented separately because the hotel check-in view can show information about the room by suitable choice of column formula. If more detail had been required, then a form would have been used.

Not shown previously are the reservation view for check-in, the stay view for check-in, and the guest details view. For these views, much more detail is required than could easily be shown in a column of a Notes view, so forms must be used. It is possible to take advantage of the Notes feature that allows a Notes view and a Notes form to share a single window. This allows a list of documents to be scanned quickly and a large amount of detail to be shown about the selected document.

Because the guest details view is to be used with both reservation and stay views, it can be implemented as a subform, which can be embedded into other forms.

6.3.2 Detailed View Design

The first thing that the clerk needs to examine in order to check in the guest is the reservation. As mentioned previously, this is implemented as a Notes view. Because the easiest item from the guest details to get from the guest is his or her name, the first column of the view is designed to show this. Putting the surname first and placing this in the first column enables the quick search facility in the view: By entering the first few characters of the name and pressing Enter, the view is scrolled to that entry. The other columns in the view allow the clerk to see the planned dates and the room type. In a more complete design there would be other information, such as frequent traveler number and special needs.

In Notes, it is not straightforward to show lists of several types of documents from the same database at the same time. We must choose among the following options:

- Place both reservations and free rooms in the same list by using a multiclause column formula to correctly show details of each type of object. You could use the column formula

@if(Form="Reservation";Surname+","+Othernames; Number)

and then use the column sorting facilities to keep the rooms and reservations apart.

- Design another view to show free rooms. Notes restricts database views so that only one may be seen in the normal window at any time. If this option is chosen, then the system either needs to switch views at appropriate times or show the view in a dialog using the @Picklist function.

- Show the free rooms in some other way, such as the allowable values in a keyword field in the stay view for check-in form once a stay document has been generated.

We decided to implement the second option. After the clerk had selected the guest's reservation, he or she would press the check-in button at the top of the view. This would create a stay based on the details from the currently selected reservation and choose one of the rooms available. To keep our designer's model correct, we split the hotel view for check-in into two: the reservations for check-in and the free rooms for check-in views. This is illustrated in Figure 6.3, where the designer's model has been changed to show the views that correspond to elements in the programmer's model. The three elements on the right of the diagram show the Notes elements in the programmer's model. The lines marked "maps to" show how the elements of the two models are related.

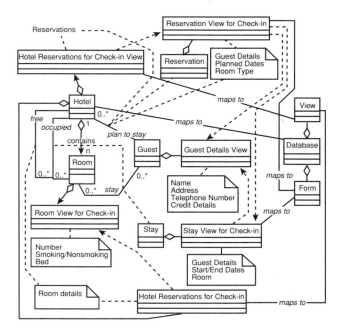

FIGURE 6.3 *Elements from both the designer's model and the programmer's model.*

The reservation view for check–in and the stay view for check–in are quite straight-forward to implement in Notes. Both can be implemented as Notes forms. The guest view for check–in is implemented as a subform, so that both the stay and reservation views are able to embed it.

6.3.3 A Hybrid Model

One of the main benefits of using a CASE tool such as Rational Rose to hold your models is that you can easily merge and combine models. This is particularly true in this stage of OVID. It is very useful to take many views of the designer's model centered on one or two objects and the associated views. If you then add to these diagrams the objects from the environment model, the mapping between elements can be discussed in detail. You will be able to consider in depth whether the users' model will be disrupted by the implementation.

The Hotel System in Notes

The screen shots shown in Figures 6.4 through 6.6 are from the hotel system, which is modeled as a Notes database.

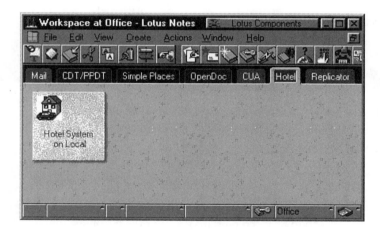

FIGURE 6.4 *A hotel database in Notes.*

View pushbuttons (called *navigators* in Notes) are provided for toggling between display of check–in and available room information. A reservation document allows entry of reservation information.

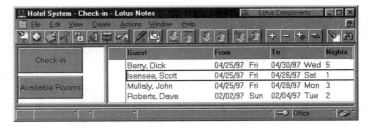

FIGURE 6.5   *The hotel check-in view.*

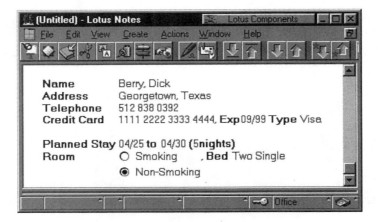

FIGURE 6.6   *A reservation form.*

6.4 Example 2: The Telephone

RealPhone was created to enable a user to use a computer as a speakerphone. In particular, it had to be designed to run on an IBM ThinkPad equipped with an MWave adapter and running the Windows 95 operating system. The implementation was to use the C++ language and to be based on the MFC. For the telephony functions there was a fixed system application programming interface (API) supplied with the hardware.

A further objective of RealPhone was to illustrate how components could be built without using rectangular windows, menu bars, and all the trappings of the current styles of graphical user interface. Instead of these things, the RealPhone would try to match a real-world telephone wherever possible. This meant that in addition to doing its job as a speakerphone, the RealPhone also had to be aesthetically appealing.

6.4.1 The Designer's Model

The development of the designer's model for RealPhone followed the four-phase, iterative process we described for the hotel system. We have not included a full description of the model and how it developed here, because it was very similar to the process for the hotel system. In this section we have focused on the processes that occurred after the construction of the designer's model, since these differed from the steps for the hotel.

When RealPhone was developed, it was decided that the views would follow a pre-defined architecture. The telephone would have two views:

- The base-function view, in which the most common tasks can be performed

- The full-function view, in which all tasks can be performed

Early design sessions continued to discuss views in terms of their fit for individual tasks. However, consolidation of these views into the two views in the architecture soon became second nature. The details of the task-based views are no longer retained in the model. This loss of information is not critical if, like RealPhone, the project is seen as a "one-off" exercise. If the same project had been seen as having a longer life, then it would be important to retain this detail for later versions.

The combination of the designer's model and the programmer's model of RealPhone is quite large. Although it is not an explicit part of the OVID methodology, we decided to use the facilities in Rational Rose to partition the model into what it calls *categories*. Membership of a particular category does not make any difference to the function of that class; it is just a convenience for administrative purposes. It allows the programmers and the designers to work on their own sections without affecting each other too much. The relationships of the categories are shown in Figure 6.7. The folderlike graphics in Figure 6.7 show categories, and the arrows show the dependencies between the categories. All classes depend on the Built in/Utility category, so, to avoid clutter, we did not show that in the figure.

A category for an answering machine is included, but this was not implemented. The categories and their roles are

- *Phone Model*—These classes are the designer's model and show how the user should think about the telephone.

- *Answering Machine Model*—The designer's model for the answering machine.

- *View*—The architecture for views.

- *Phone FFV*—The designer's model of the full-function view of the telephone.

- *Answering Machine FFV*—The designer's model of the full-function view of the answering machine.

- *Display for FFV*—The designer's model of the components shared between the full-function views of the telephone and answering machine.

- *TAPI*—The programmer's model of the Telephony API, which is a standard interface for connection to the telephony hardware.

- *Line Model*—The programmer's model for classes that adapt the telephony functions.

- *Built in/Utility*—The programmer's model for the services provided by C++ and MFC.

- *Controls*—The programmer's model of abstractly defined controls, which provide views of individual attributes or commands.

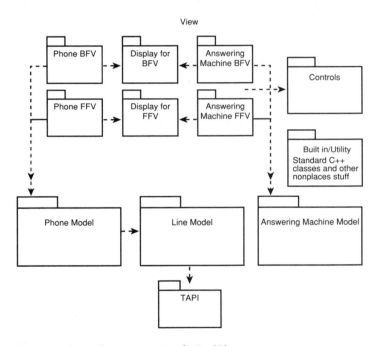

FIGURE 6.7 *Category overview for RealPhone.*

The class diagram for the phone model category (Figure 6.8) shows the objects of which the user is aware. The diagram does not show the detail of the connection between the telephone and line. The diagram shows that one single view will take the role of current view. This will be either a base-function view or a full-function view, depending on the user's selection. In Figure 6.8, the names in parentheses after the class name indicate which categories each class comes from. Where no name is shown, that class is part of the phone model category. The telephone view at the top center of the figure represents both the base-function view and the full-function view, so the details are not shown here.

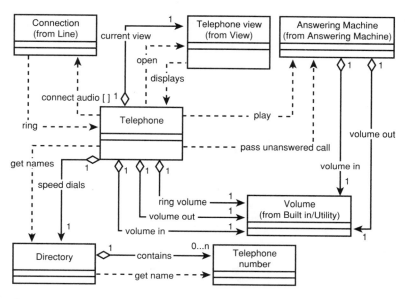

FIGURE 6.8   *The main view from the telephone model category.*

The base function view of the telephone comes from the Phone BFV category and shows how this view is decomposed into smaller units. For example, in Figure 6.9, because the speed dial field view was used by both views, it was modeled in the phone FFV category. The handset view, which shows the line state, is also shared, but it was modeled in this category.

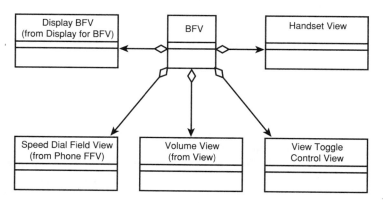

FIGURE 6.9   *The containment diagram for base-function view of the telephone.*

6.4.2 The Environment Model

As you have seen, the programmer's model, which includes the model of the environment, is contained in some of the categories of the larger phone model. One of the first elements to be documented was the Telephony API, or TAPI. The TAPI model has a big influence on the facilities that can be offered to the user and allows those building the designer's model to consider this at an appropriate time. (See Figure 6.10.) In Figure 6.10, the state model was derived from reading the TAPI specification. The transitions shown are those documented in the specification. Notice that this is an incomplete model because many of the states have no exit conditions. This is typical of a model that has been documented in prose.

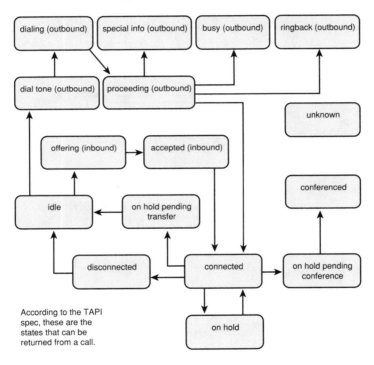

FIGURE 6.10   *The state model of the TAPI telephone line.*

6.4.3 Decomposing the Designer's Model

For RealPhone, the decomposition of the designer's model was mostly concerned with providing more details of the views and how they were built. The decomposition was done in terms of the abstract property views in the Controls category. (See Figure 6.11.)

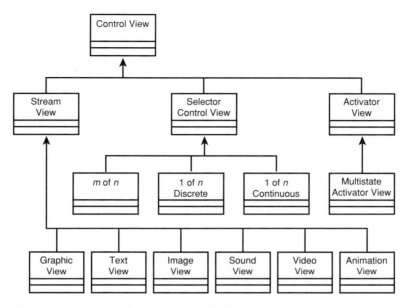

FIGURE 6.11   *An inheritance diagram for abstract property views.*

In Figure 6.11 these controls provide a classification of the various types of property so that the mapping to real controls can be made. The terms used in the figure are our classification of the elementary views: Stream classes allow for data input and output; activator classes cause actions or commands to happen; selectors allow the user to choose between the possible states of an object.

Each property or command was mapped to one of these classes. The effect of this mapping is to define the freedoms for the graphics and programming design of forms and windows. Most of the classes in the controls category can be mapped to several programming constructs or to individually designed views. For example, the 1 of *n* discrete class could be implemented as a group of radio buttons, a drop-down combination box, a drop-down list, or some special graphic. The choice among these can be made in order to fit with stylistic or practical considerations in the design. For example, for RealPhone we wanted a style that looked like a real-world object, so a specially designed view was chosen.

Having an abstract control defined for each element of the model helps when a design might be used in several contexts. Different mappings can be produced to the programming elements to fit with the needs of an implementation. If a more traditional design were needed for a telephone, it would be quite simple to map the abstract controls to real controls (radio buttons, check boxes, and so on) rather than special graphical elements.

6.4.4 Prototypes of the Views

One of the important phases in the design of RealPhone was prototyping of views. The first versions of the prototype were drawn on small pieces of paper so that they could be combined in various ways, and then they were used to run through the scenarios of use for the telephone. (See Figure 6.12.)

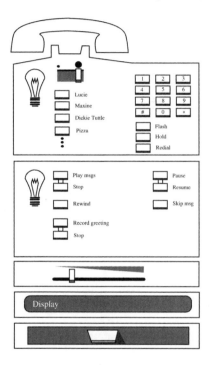

FIGURE 6.12 *An early prototype of RealPhone.*

As we stepped through each task, it was possible to see whether the appropriate information was available to the user and whether the controls were accessible.

Having reached agreement at this level, a very clear specification was available to the programmers and designers who implemented the RealPhone. The implementation went though several phases, with two different graphics styles being used at various stages. A beta program, which gathered comments, evaluated these by email and telephone (one of the speed dial buttons was programmed to call the comment line). The most significant change applied from the beta program was to increase the number of speed dial buttons from 5 to 10. The final version of RealPhone is shown in Figures 6.13 through 6.15.

FIGURE 6.13 *RealPhone in base-function view.*

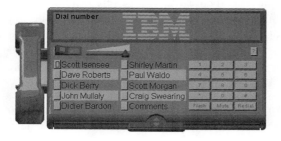

FIGURE 6.14 *RealPhone in full-function view.*

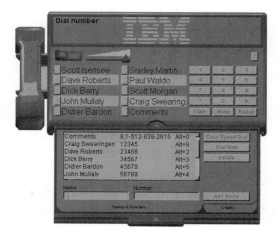

FIGURE 6.15 *RealPhone in full-function view with drawer extended.*

6.5 Conclusion

Development of the designer's model should be entirely user driven. Data from the users and about the users should control each decision. In contrast, the implementation of the designer's model as a programmer's model varies from case to case. It is driven by implementation requirements, such as the platform on which the system will run and the style that the customer requires. Until development of the programmer's model, OVID is independent of the implementation platform. It can be used with any operating system and GUI style, including, as demonstrated with the RealPhone, entirely new styles.

The segregation of concerns, which OVID provides, can be very helpful to the design team. Knowing which of the two models an element belongs to can give you the discipline to make each decision from the best perspective. If an element is in the designer's model, then the question is always What is best for the user? If an element belongs to the programmer's model, the question becomes What is the best way to make this work?

OVID allows the development process to flow smoothly from interface design to implementation. It eliminates the traditional "throw it over the wall" disconnect between phases.

PART III

Supporting Tasks

CHAPTER 7

Prototyping

- **Prototyping techniques**
  Both high- and low-fidelity prototypes have their place in the development process. High-fidelity prototypes are fully interactive. Low-fidelity prototypes are limited-function and limited-interaction prototypes.

- **Managing iteration**
  Prototyping is an iterative process that evolves to increasingly better designs. Criteria should be set to determine when a design is good enough.

A prototype is a model of an application. It simulates the user interface and important functions of the program being modeled. Isensee and Rudd (1996) identify the major advantages of prototyping as

- Better collection of customer requirements

- Cost saving

- Increased quality

- Evaluation of new interface techniques and functions

- Demonstration of feasibility

- Use as a sales tool

- Definition of clear specification

- Allowance of early testing

- Demonstration of early progress

- User satisfaction

- Better design

7.1 Reasons to Prototype

The use of prototypes as an aid in customer requirements collection is particularly important in an iterative development methodology such as OVID. Waterfall design methodologies required that the clients or end users have a clear idea of what they want a program to do and how they want it implemented, but users rarely have this level of understanding and vision. They just know that they have a problem and seek an expert to design a solution. Boar (1984) reports that 20% to 40% of all system problems can be traced to problems in the design process, and 60% to 80% can be traced to inaccurate requirements definitions. The cost to correct an error in a program increases dramatically as the life cycle progresses, so it is critical to catch errors in requirements and design before coding starts. (See Figure 7.1.)

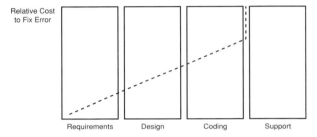

Relative Cost to Fix Error

Requirements   Design   Coding   Support

F IGURE   7 . 1   *A graph of the increasing cost of fixing an error (adapted from Snyder 1991).*

Note

If you don't prototype, problems may not be noticed until the product is in the hands of your customers. The later problems are caught, the more difficult and expensive they are to fix. Many well-known product failures, such as New Coke, Fab One-Shot, the smokeless cigarette, and the PC Junior have been due to inadequate customer feedback during product development.

OVID uses prototypes throughout the development cycle to continually verify customer requirements and test that the interface under development is meeting those requirements. User interface prototypes are very valuable as long as they are conducted in a disciplined requirements management process so that closure is ensured.

7.2 Prototyping Techniques

7.2.1 Low–Fidelity Prototypes

Low-fidelity prototypes are limited-function and limited-interaction prototypes. They are constructed to depict concepts, design alternatives, and screen layouts rather than to model the user interaction with a system. Low-fidelity prototypes are constructed quickly and provide limited or no functionality.

Some people ask, "Doesn't it take almost as much work to build a prototype as to make the final system?" The answer lies in Pareto's Law. It takes only a small amount of effort to produce much of what is wanted, whereas a large amount of additional effort is required to produce exactly what is wanted. It is generally possible to obtain a large amount of the most important capability of the system after implementing only a small part of the system. Effective prototyping requires that you determine and model only the key aspects of the user interface. (See Figure 7.2.)

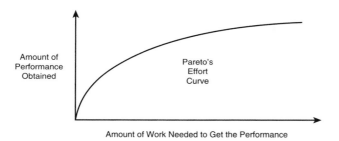

FIGURE 7.2 *The curve of Pareto's Law.*

Users do not exercise a low-fidelity prototype to get a firsthand idea of how it operates; rather, low-fidelity prototypes are demonstrated by someone skilled at operating or explaining the prototype. Low-fidelity prototypes are used early in the design cycle to show general conceptual approaches without much investment in development.

We use two forms of low-fidelity prototype in OVID: abstract and concrete.

Abstract prototypes serve as a communication vehicle between the interface designer and visual designer. The designer's model is translated into views, which are represented in an abstract form. For example, the abstract prototype for the RealPhone shown in Figure 7.3 represents the controls in block diagram form. The interface designer can use this prototype to communicate the design to the rest of the team.

The visual designer works from the abstract prototype and produces drawings of the interface as a concrete low-fidelity prototype. This level of prototype is more easily understood by end users than the abstract version. (See Figure 7.4.)

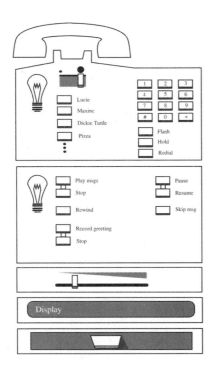

FIGURE 7.3   *An example of an abstract low-fidelity prototype.*

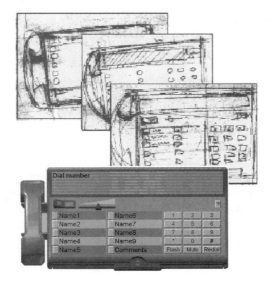

FIGURE 7.4   *An example of a concrete low-fidelity prototype—progressing from sketches to a 3D model.*

7.2.2 High–Fidelity Prototypes

High-fidelity prototypes are fully interactive. Users can enter data, respond to messages, open windows, and, in general, interact with the prototype just as they would a real application.

High-fidelity prototypes trade off speed for accuracy. They are not as quick and easy to create as low-fidelity prototypes, but they faithfully represent the interface to be implemented in the product. They can be made so realistic that the user cannot distinguish them from the actual product.

High-fidelity prototypes are invaluable for usability testing. Whereas low–fidelity prototypes address the layout and visuals of an interface (surface presentation), high-fidelity prototypes address the issues of navigation and flow. The users can operate the prototype as they would the real product. Windows can be opened and data entered. Messages are delivered at appropriate times. Data can be displayed in real-time and the user can take action in response to the data. Errors and deviations from the expected path can be flagged and identified to the user as if using a real product. (See Figure 7.5.) The user can get a sense of how the product will operate and can make informed recommendations about how to improve the user interface. Usability testing can be conducted early in the design process with the prototype as a test vehicle.

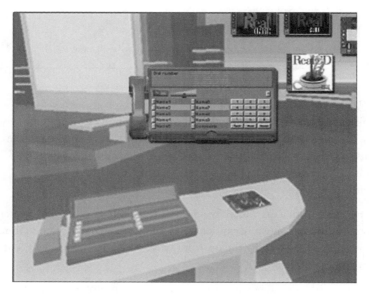

FIGURE 7.5 *An example of a high-fidelity prototype—fully interactive.*

7.2.3 Comparison

Both high- and low-fidelity prototypes have their place in the development process. Table 7.1 compares the advantages and disadvantages of each to help in choosing which is most appropriate for a given situation on your interface design project.

TABLE 7.1 COMPARISON OF HIGH- AND LOW-FIDELITY PROTOTYPES.

Advantages	Disadvantages
Low-Fidelity Prototype	
Lower development cost	Limited error checking
Evaluate multiple design concepts	Poorly detailed specification for coding
Useful communication vehicle	Facilitator driven
Address screen layout issues	Limited utility after requirements established
Useful for identifying market requirements	Limitations in usability testing
Proof of concept	Navigational and flow limitations
High-Fidelity Prototype	
High degree of functionality	More expensive to develop
Fully interactive	Time-consuming to create
User driven	Inefficient for proof of concept designs
Clearly defines navigational scheme	Not effective for requirements gathering
Useful for exploration and testing	
Look and feel of final product	
A living specification	
Marketing and sales tool	

7.3 Managing Iteration

The prototyping effort needs to be bounded. It can be tempting to continue revising the design and generating new prototypes without end. To be successful, the prototype must converge toward a better design at a reasonable rate of speed and cost. The goals of the prototype can be specified in terms of usability criteria. Progress toward those goals can be measured by usability tests.

User requirements and a first-pass interface design are required before prototyping begins. Prototypes are not a replacement for up-front design work. Trying to iterate until you get it right without doing the up-front work is not only inefficient, but can lead to uncontrolled iteration.

Collins (1995) describes several possible paths that iterative prototyping may take with respect to design goals. Figure 7.6 shows the ideal iterative process. This assumes that there is an ideal solution in the space of possible designs and a succession of prototypes spirals into it. By measuring the usability characteristics of the design at each iteration and modifying the prototype to address problems, each iteration comes closer to the goal. Unproductive iteration is avoided, minimizing time and cost.

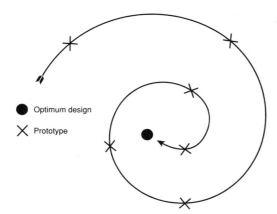

FIGURE 7.6 *An idealized view of iterative design.*

Often, however, multiple designs are equally good. For certain features, one design may be optimum. As you prototype other parts of the application, or add to the prototype, the optimum design may change. This can cause the prototypes to wander unproductively and perhaps never converge. This can be avoided by prototyping the most important (e.g., most critical, most frequently performed) functions first and not significantly changing the design for less important functions. Another strategy is to create a broad, horizontal prototype, which represents most of the user interface for the product. (See Figure 7.7.)

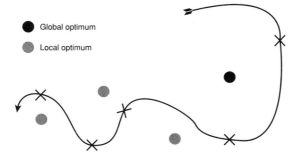

FIGURE 7.7 *An iteration around multiple optimal designs.*

A prime cause of wandering iteration is not having a good conceptual model of the system. This forces developers to evaluate designs in a haphazard way. Trial and error is a very inefficient design technique.

Another potential problem with iteration is when designs circle the optimum without clear improvement. Many alternative designs are prototyped, but no one can agree whether the new solution is better or worse. This situation typically occurs when the project does not have usability goals and accurate measurements. (See Figure 7.8.)

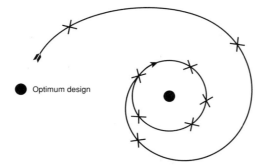

FIGURE 7.8   *When iteration fails to converge.*

Chapter 8, "Evaluation," discusses techniques for evaluating the user interface.

CHAPTER **8**

Evaluation

- **Reasons for conducting user evaluations**
  Without user testing, products would reach the market untried and may fail
  due to problems that could have been identified and fixed during development.

- **Types of user evaluations**
  User evaluations can be conducted as field evaluations, walkthroughs, or
  lab tests.

- **Performing a usability lab test**
  Usability testing is crucial to the success of a project. Such testing involves
  designing the experiment, selecting participants, developing tasks, preparing
  materials, collecting and analyzing data, and conducting postmortem evaluations.

8.1 Reasons for Conducting User Evaluations

User evaluations are conducted to identify problems users will have with software in
all facets of its use: installing, learning, operating, customizing, and so forth.
Without user testing, products would reach the market untried and may fail due to
problems that could have been identified and fixed during development.

Evaluations that are conducted during design of a product are referred to as *formative
evaluations*. Formative evaluations guide a development team in producing products
that are usable and useful.

Evaluations that take place after a product has been developed are referred to as
summative because they are concerned with making judgments about a completed

product. These are typically run to make sure a product meets certain criteria before it ships.

Preece et al. (1994) identify the following reasons for doing evaluations:

- *Understanding the real world.* It is important to determine whether a design can be improved to fit the work environment better. This kind of activity is particularly important during requirements gathering and then later, for ensuring that prototypes of the system fulfill users' needs.

- *Comparing designs.* Which is best? There are various occasions when designers want to compare two or more designs or design ideas. For example, early in the design process there may be debate about which way to implement a particular function. An evaluation may be conducted to empirically determine which one works best.

- *Engineering toward a target.* Is it good enough? The design process can be viewed as a form of engineering. The designers have a target, which is often expressed as some form of metric, and their goal is to make sure their design produces a product that meets the criteria. For example, the product may need to be better than competing products in order to be viable.

8.2 Types of User Evaluations

Different types of evaluations are conducted at different points in the development cycle, depending on the type of information most needed at each point. In general, evaluations in the early stages of the development cycle are quick, informal, and frequent. Evaluations later in the cycle tend to be longer and more formal.

During requirements gathering, evaluations are conducted to determine the needs of the users for which the system will be designed. As design of the interface starts, design alternatives are tested to make sure they work adequately or to find out which one of several alternatives works best. As design of the interface is completed, evaluations determine whether design criteria have been met. Different kinds of evaluations may be carried out at different stages of the design for different reasons, but the role of the evaluation is always to verify and improve the design.

8.2.1 Field Evaluation

Field evaluations (see Figure 8.1) are common at both the beginning and the end of the development cycle. At the beginning of the cycle, they are used to collect customer requirements. Users are observed performing the tasks the system will automate or replace. User requirements are elicited through interviews or questionnaires.

FIGURE 8.1 *An example of a field evaluation.*

Late in the development cycle, field tests are performed to validate the earlier lab testing. They verify that the lab results were representative of actual field performance.

Field Evaluation in Designing a Hotel Application

In evaluating a hotel application, we would visit a representative sample of hotels early in the project. We would talk to the desk clerks, managers, and any others who will use the system to understand their needs. We would review the system they are currently using and observe the tasks they perform.

Later in the project, after we have a version of the system and a prototype running, we would visit hotels again to observe our new system being used under real field conditions with representative users.

8.2.2 Walkthrough/Inspection

A walkthrough (see Figure8.2) is an informal verification of the interface. The evaluators step through a set of tasks to exercise the interface. They make sure the interface works as designed and look for any obvious usability problems.

FIGURE 8.2 *An example of a walkthrough/inspection.*

> **Walking Through the Hotel Application**
>
> Once we have the first prototype or initial version of the hotel interface working, we walk through each of the tasks the system is to support to ensure that they are working properly. Taking this step can help us avoid spending the time and money to perform longer and more formal evaluations if the application is not working correctly.

8.2.3 Formal Lab Testing

Formal lab testing (see Figure 8.3) is the most rigorous form of evaluation. It typically employs experimental design methodology to measure user performance with the interface in a manner that allows statistical comparisons to be made and conclusions to be drawn.

FIGURE 8.3   *An example of a formal lab test.*

> **Performing Lab Testing on the Hotel Application**
>
> After we have verified that the system is working with the walkthrough, we run the hotel system through a formal laboratory test. This catches the majority of the system's usability problems and enables us to estimate the frequency and severity of each so that we can prioritize them for repair. At this point, we recruit participants; they are representative of the hotel staff in key characteristics such as computer experience, but they do not necessarily have to be the actual users of the final system.

8.3 How to Perform a Usability Lab Test

The following sections cover the basics of usability testing, which is crucial to the success of a project. For more comprehensive coverage, consult texts devoted to this topic, such as Nielsen and Mack (1994) or Hix and Hartson (1993).

Lab tests are performed in an environment where accurate measurements can be taken and conditions can be controlled to reduce or eliminate interruptions, noise, and other factors that would contaminate the data. Figure 8.4 shows a typical usability laboratory. Test participants work on their own in one room. Observers monitor the test participants from an adjacent room using a one-way mirror and/or video cameras.

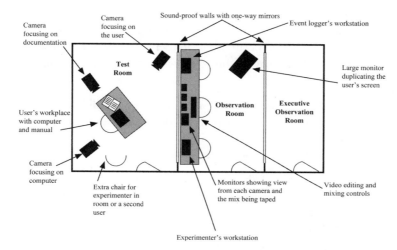

FIGURE 8.4 *The floor plan of a typical usability laboratory (Nielsen 1993).*

8.3.1 Designing the Experiment

You must first decide the purpose of the test and then design an appropriate experiment. As in all experimentation, you must control the conditions and measure the results. Decisions to be made when designing the experiment include

- Goals of the test
- Number and description of test participants
- Testing schedule
- Testing method
- Tasks to be performed
- Measures to be collected
- Data analysis techniques to be used
- How to report the results and what actions to take based on these results

8.3.2 Selecting Participants

The type of participants you select depends on the purpose of the test. For example, if you are trying to predict performance expected in the general population, your sample should be representative of the population. If you are concerned about identifying problems that novice users may have using your product, then you should bring in novice users for the test.

You will typically want users who are knowledgeable in a particular domain. For example, an interface to be used by tellers in a bank should be tested on people with bank teller experience. Test participants without this domain knowledge may have errors that would not be likely to occur in a valid user population. Participants with the proper domain knowledge may be able to give you valuable suggestions on improving your product.

You will generally want a participant group with a mixture of skill levels. Novices may trip over problems that experts would breeze right past without noticing. Experts may find subtle problems (e.g., small inconsistencies and nonoptimum navigation) that novices would never notice.

The number of participants should be determined based on the analyses to be conducted. For statistical comparisons, power analyses are available to determine the number of subjects needed to find statistically significant results given certain values of key parameters. Nielsen and Molich (1990) find the optimum number of participants to be three to five per user class. Smaller samples miss problems or are too heavily influenced by a single participant, whereas larger samples may not be worth the diminishing returns obtained.

The graph in Figure 8.5, adapted from Nielsen and Mack (1994), shows the curve of diminishing returns in proportion of problems identified as sample size increases.

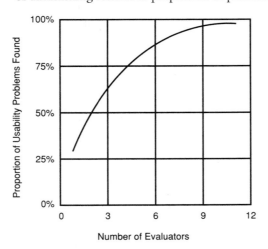

FIGURE 8.5 *Graph of the number of core usability problems found (Nielsen and Mack 1994).*

Landauer (1995) graphs the cost/benefit ratio of usability testing as the number of tests or number or evaluators increases. (See Figure 8.6.)

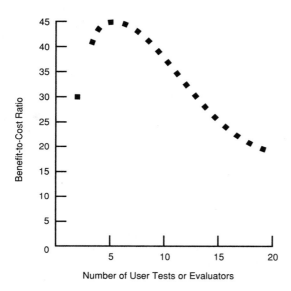

FIGURE 8.6   *The benefit-to-cost ratio of usability testing.*

You may occasionally want to use participants for more than one test condition or for repetitions of a given test. This may increase test efficiency, but it introduces potential biases.

8.3.3 Developing Tasks

A set of benchmark tasks should be developed where user performance can be compared against the goals that have been set for the project. Other representative tasks are added to ensure that all important functions and areas of the application are evaluated. In early phases of the development cycle, the task list may be short, exercising only the functions available in the prototype at the time or those that are most frequent or important. In the later stages of development, the task list must be comprehensive enough to evaluate all significant areas of the product. Some examples of tasks for the hotel reservation system include

- Record a reservation
- Check in a customer
- View a room cleaning list
- Generate a day-end financial report

8.3.4 Preparing Materials

Materials need to be developed to support the test. These materials may include:

- *The prototype.* You must have some form of prototype of the system for the users to operate. The prototype must be capable of performing the scenarios you are interested in testing. You may have to enter particular data into the prototype and reset it after each participant.

- *Background questionnaire.* The backgrounds of the participants may influence their performance. It is useful to have questionnaires to collect this data in case it is needed in later analysis.

- *Experimenter instructions.* You should carefully list all the steps the experimenter should perform during the test. You want to make sure you don't forget any steps in the rush of running the experiment, and you want the procedure to be consistent from one participant to the next. You may have assistants, and you will want them to follow the same procedure.

- *Participant instructions.* Participants should be given enough information to understand what tasks they should perform, but not so much that you lead them toward a particular way of performing the task. In general, these instructions should be expressed in terms of goals rather than procedures.

- *Data collection forms.* You should have forms tailored to the data you want to collect so that you can record results as quickly as possible without making errors or losing track of what the participant is doing. Significant events often happen quickly and one after another. Many labs use data logging software, which can collect and then summarize the data. Data may also be synchronized with video recording equipment to allow you to easily review significant events from the test.

- *Video and audio taping equipment.* It is often helpful to record the test. If the experimenter misses something in real-time, he or she can go back to the tape to review the event. Video summaries can be very persuasive in convincing people who were not at the test that a problem exists. Typically at least two cameras are used: one to capture what happens on the screen and the other to capture users' actions. Scan converters can record activity on the computer screen direct to videotape without requiring a camera.

- *Confidentiality and permission forms.* If you don't want test participants talking about your product outside the company, you need to warn them that the information is confidential and have them sign a form agreeing to this. You should also have a form for them to sign acknowledging that they are aware that they are being recorded and allowing you to use these recordings and other results of the test in your report.

- *Posttest interview list.* Prepare a list of questions to ask and points to go over at the end of the test. You may want to ask the participants for their opinions on the product and specific aspects of it, ask questions about some of their actions in the test, and ask them to clarify comments they made during the test.

8.3.5 Data Collection

Test conditions should be controlled as carefully as possible to prevent extraneous effects such as differences in instructions or stimuli to influence the results. A uniform set of introductory remarks should be delivered to participants. These remarks typically include instructions stating that the purpose of the session is to evaluate the system, not themselves.

Common measures for a usability test are performance in terms of time and errors and satisfaction. The performance measures can be collected through observation or by instrumenting the prototype. Data logging programs are available for entry and classification of data.

Tests are often videotaped to allow the experimenter the opportunity to review events that happen quickly and may not be adequately understood or documented in real-time. The video usually includes an audio record of the testing, which is known as a "verbal protocol" (Ericsson and Simon 1985). A verbal protocol provides a wide range of information, such as the way a user plans to do a particular task, his or her identification of interface objects, and the level of understanding of messages. This audio information captures subtle cues, such as comments or tone of voice, that aren't captured in other measurements but can be important clues in understanding the reasons behind users' actions.

A form of verbal protocol frequently used is a "think aloud protocol." The user is asked to say out loud what he or she is thinking as a task is performed. This is very helpful in understanding the reasons for user errors. A drawback is that it is difficult for users to talk while performing the task without distracting them and consequently having a negative impact on task performance.

Interviews and questionnaires should be used to collect information about the backgrounds and experience levels of test participants. They can also be helpful after a test to elicit user comments about the design and additional information needed to understand why the users did what they did during the test.

8.3.6 Data Analysis

Statistical data analysis techniques are recommended whenever you have sufficient sample size and quantitative data. These techniques allow you to judge which effects are statistically significant versus those that are weak enough that they may be attributable to chance variations. Comparisons may be made against benchmark goals or competing products, or between design alternatives.

Whether the test is large or small, the amount of data collected in a usability test can seem overwhelming. It helps to organize the analysis into steps and proceed methodically, so that each piece is of a manageable size and so you don't miss anything. One way to segment this is to look at the data one task at a time. Focus on identifying problems first, and then go back and develop solutions.

Results are commonly delivered in a report listing the problems, frequency of occurrence, severity, and recommended solutions. Time, error, satisfaction, and any other measures you have collected can be compared against the usability goals you have set. The report is often supplemented with a videotape documenting significant events in the testing.

8.3.7 Postmortem Evaluation

Postmortem evaluations are often held to review the reasons for success or failure of a project. They help to determine how the process can be improved in the future. The postmortem review is conducted by the key members of the development team. A moderator, who was not part of the project, often runs the postmortem evaluation. This review is often supplemented by *postship data*, which measures performance of the product in the field.

CHAPTER 9

Conclusions

- **The OVID methodology**
  The OVID methodology is user centered. OVID provides a methodology for designing user interfaces based upon user input. It advocates design by a mulitdisciplinary team and is an end-to-end process covering requirements collection to implementation.

OVID is a design method that focuses team development of products on a common design language. It is a rigorous method, which applies engineering principles to an area generally treated more as an art than a science. It is a method that is ideally suited to modern user interfaces and component-based development—a growing trend in the industry.

This method makes use of models to build software that is easy to learn and use. Input from task analysis is used to create class, task, and state diagrams. From these diagrams, the interface and visual designers produce designs of the views, and the programming team designs the implementation code.

The usability of a system is not skin deep. To achieve a usable system, it is usually not sufficient for the externals of the user interface to be well designed; the underlying functionality of the system must be defined and organized in a way that makes it usable. The users' and designer's models must be congruent. OVID guides the interface designer in determining the user's model and developing the designer's model.

9.1 The OVID Methodology

The OVID methodology is user centered. The primary goal of a user interface should be to meet users' needs. The interface should be effective for users to perform their tasks, quick and easy to learn and use, flexible enough to cope with changes in tasks, and satisfying or even fun.

Users are involved in the design process from start to finish. They supply requirements and task definitions, participate on the design team, and evaluate the design through usability testing. The design process is iterative, with feedback from user tests and prototypes feeding into redesigns to resolve usability problems. It is difficult for a designer to accurately predict what will be usable. Many usability problems are based on misunderstandings, and designers cannot forget all they know in order to put themselves in the user's shoes and see the design in ways the user might. Involvement by real users is essential.

Designs produced using OVID utilize objects. The objects used in the system are familiar to users because they are derived from their mental models. User tasks are expressed in terms of actions on these objects. This produces an intuitive and flexible interface. We often find that the system accommodates new or unusual tasks that were not even identified in the original task analysis.

OVID leads to a concise definition of the designer's model. This model is independent of the style of the user interface—both the platform style (e.g., Windows, Macintosh, UNIX) and object or task orientation. Our focus on objects tends to make an object-oriented interface a natural result, but also ensures that the objects presented in task-oriented user interfaces have clearly defined and useful distinctions for users and therefore that the tasks are unambiguous.

OVID moves design on the continuum from art toward science. There remains, however, much need for creativity and good judgment. There is no "perfect" interface design and no cookbook method that guarantees good design. This process is a tool, and, as with any tool, it must be used intelligently to be effective.

OVID is customizable. You may not always be able to apply the complete methodology, but following even parts of it should help you along the way to a better design. Considerations in how much of OVID to use include the size and complexity of the software you are designing; the amount of time you have to design; and the skills, expertise, and experience of the design team. The more you have of any of these, the more OVID will be able to help you.

OVID is continuing to evolve, as are the tools available and the nature of user interfaces. We will be adapting OVID for the Web and other environments. We hope you have found this book useful, and we are interested in your feedback. Comments

can be sent via email to isensee@us.ibm.com. Watch our Web sites at
http://www.ibm.com/easy (Figure 9.1) and http:// www.ibm.com/hci for updated
information on OVID and other user-interface projects we are working on.

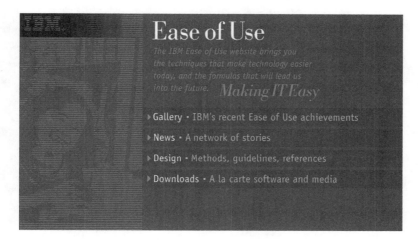

FIGURE 9.1 *The IBM Ease of Use Web site.*

We hope that you have as much fun, challenge, and satisfaction designing user interfaces as we do!

PART **IV**

Appendixes

APPENDIX A

OVID Case Study:
IBM RealCD

IBM RealCD is a good example of OVID in action. (See Figure A.1.) The RealCD project utilized OVID throughout the design process, from task analysis through a few iterations of objects, views, and interaction design. It is also a good example because the object model itself is relatively simple and easy to grasp for the purpose of this study. The relatively simple object model makes the object diagrams easy to see and comprehend in their entirety, which helps demonstrate the value of modeling and allows you to focus on the other important details of the OVID process and the progression of the design.

FIGURE A.1 *IBM RealCD.*

Through requirements gathering and analysis for this project, an understanding of users' conceptual models was applied to formulate a designer's model of the system. The designer's model was formulated by finding the key objects identified in task analysis. Also according to task analysis, views were identified to support key task groupings. Using Rational Rose, the resulting developer's model was recorded as an abstract object model diagram, and this model was refined through iteration. Iteration included decomposition and further definition of the model, in conjunction with definition of task flow and state diagrams. Soon the designer's model was fully object, state, and task flow diagrams, and visual design was done. From there, the designer's model was converted to an implementation with relative ease, and further refinements were done through prototyping and testing the design.

The figures used to illustrate the various stages of the design methodology are from the actual working documents of the project. Therefore, there are some idiosyncrasies specific to the RealCD project, but the materials serve to demonstrate OVID in practice. All these materials were very useful in the initial definition, review, refinement, and delivery of the design to the development team. The administration of the project was facilitated as much as the design itself by the structured approach provided by OVID.

A.1 Project Background

As you will see, RealCD does not have the typical user interface style, which includes window frames, title bars, and menu bars. It was one of the objectives of the RealCD project to explore an exciting new interface style based on visually rich and highly realistic metaphors. Another objective was to explore Java as an implementation platform. The task-oriented objective was to provide an interface to audio CDs played on a computer.

Whereas OVID was very effective in achieving these objectives, the methodology in no way favors one particular style of interface or implementation platform over another. The abstract modeling of OVID serves to accommodate any style and incorporate whatever product objectives there may be for a design.

All objectives, initial plans, and milestones were recorded as a database in Lotus Notes. Notes then served as a repository for all project materials, including notes and formalized documentation from task analysis, competitive analysis, and numerous diagrams and tables generated from the object model. The tool used for documenting the object model was Rational Rose.

A.2 Task Analysis

Task analysis was conducted with a combination of methods. First was a focus group discussion, which provided input on task requirements and indications of a clear object model for CDs themselves, their contents, and their associated information. It also became evident that the users' conceptual models of the relationships between CDs and CD players were somewhat confused by the relationships of CD to computer, computer to player, and CD to player.

This input helped us generate an initial list of tasks to be supported, as well as a list of essential objects. (It is interesting that the concept of a separate object such as "player" was not considered essential.) We then proceeded with the innovative concept of providing a CD object that can actually play itself.

At the same time, we provided a questionnaire to approximately 1,000 people among the students, staff, and faculty of a university. Without any reference to using computers, we asked questions about how they listen to music. The feedback from this questionnaire, as well as some competitive analysis, helped us prioritize the various tasks related to listening to audio CDs. (See Figure A.2.)

After analyzing the task data, we documented a prioritized list of tasks to be supported and a simple object model. Both were subsequently further defined in an iterative manner. Through further analysis, we broke down tasks into individual steps for performing each task. Eventually our list of task requirements was refined to a detailed list of user actions to be supported. (See Figure A.3.)

#	Task	Priority
1	Just Play	1
2	Play Specified Track (SPECIFY TRACK)	1
3	Play Playlist (SPECIFY PLAYLIST)	2
4	Play from Specified Track (& continue)	1
5	Play in random order (SET RANDOM)	2
6	Play continuously	2
7	Play from current position	1
8	Play fast	
9	Play in reverse	
10	Play slow	
11	Stop (& keep position)	1
12	Stop & return to beginning	1
13	Just stop	1
14	Stop & hold place (w/ persistence)	
15	Change to specified track	1
a	step through (as per fwd)	
b	redo playlist	
c	direct access	
16	Go to next	1
16B	Go forward (on same track)	1
16C	Go backward (on same track)	1
17	Go to previous	1
18	Start over (track)	1
19	Start over (CD, playlist)	1
20	Eject CD	1
21	Adjust volume	1
22	Adjust balance	4
23	Adjust bass	4
24	Adjust treble	4
25	View levels (left/right)	4
26	View CD name/art/times	2
27	View track name/art	2
28	View track time	3
29	View (track) timer	1
30	View (track/CD) time remaining	2
31	View playlist	2
32	Change playlist	2
33	View something else (e.g., desktop, other stuff, etc.) (MOVE, SIZE, minimize)	1
34	Hide	1
35	Put away	1
36	Minimize	1
37	Store	4
38	Copy (e.g., music off of CD)	
39	Send to someone	
40	Play at specific time	
41	Stop at specific time	
42	Stop on cue (upon event)	(4)
43	Keep somewhere (CD view)	4
43b	Copy (CD view)	4
44	Get rid of (CD view)	4
45	View liner notes	
46	View other CD info	3

FIGURE A.2   *A prioritized list of tasks to be supported.*

User Action	Description
Play	Play playlist from current position according to play settings
Pause	Pause
Stop	Stop playing, set current position to beginning of 1st track in play list
Track forward	Go to next track in playlist unless at last track. If Continuous Play is On, then loop around.
Position forward	Advance position within the current track until the end.
Track backward	If current position <10 seconds into track, go to previous track in playlist unless at first track in playlist. If >10 seconds, go to beginning of current track. If then loop around.
Position backward	Rewind position within the current track until the beginning
Eject	Open CD drive to eject CD
Switch Views	Change view to specified view
Put Away	Shut down ("Close") RealCD object (& book)
Put AwayBook	Close RealCD book and put back in CD case
Minimize	Minimize RealCD window to task bar (note task bar limitations for Java)
Set Random. On/Off	Randomizes Playlist / Resets Playlist
Set Continuous On/Off	Loop Play back / Don't Loop
Set Current Track	Sets current track directly to a specific track in playlist
Set Track On/Off	Sets Track On/Off in the playlist
Reposition Track	Repositions Tracks within the playlist
Adjust audio out	Launches Win95 Volume control
Move CD	Moves RealCD window (and Book window when appropriate)
Edit CD title	Edit-in-place text, updates all CD title labels
Edit Track title	Edit-in-place text, updates all title labels for that track
Move Book	Moves Book window
Open Book	Opens cover of book in place
Close Book	Closes book in place
Turn page	Turns to next page in sequence away from the spine
Add tracks to playlist	Ejects disc, prompts for next disc, appends tracks to current playlist
Reset Playlist Order	Resets Playlist order to original (that on CD itself)
Select CD Clip Art	Assign artwork to CD Cover, CD Spine, Book Cover, …
Customize CD Art	Note: done through Windows…replacing content of CD folder in Library

FIGURE A.3 *Detailed user actions.*

A.3 Project Design

A.3.1 Object Design

Object design begins with identifying key objects from users' conceptual models, as discovered through task analysis. As mentioned previously, user input for the RealCD project indicated a clear object model for CDs themselves, their contents, and their associated information. It also indicated that the users' models of the relationships between CDs and CD players were somewhat confused by the relationships of CD to computer, computer to player, and CD to player. This input helped us generate an initial list of essential objects.

The object model was begun with just a few essential objects. In task analysis, although the usage of terms such as *CD*, *disc*, *playlist*, and *tracks* sometimes overlapped, it became clear that these really represented four different concepts that formed the core of the object model. (See Figure A.4.)

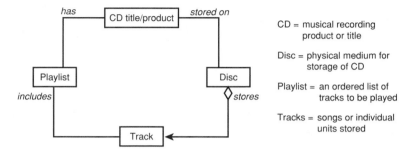

FIGURE A.4 *The initial object model for an audio CD.*

Building on the initial model, a more detailed designer's model was defined to include nested objects, relationships between those objects, and initial views. (See Figure A.5.)

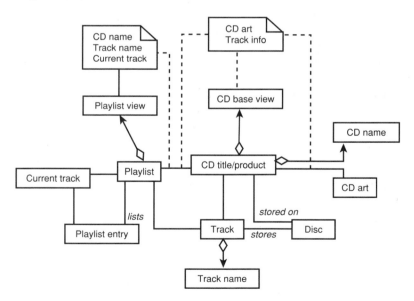

FIGURE A.5 *A more detailed object model, including views.*

A.3.2 View Design

View design is also driven for the most part by task analysis. As the object model is defined, views are identified to accommodate key groupings of tasks and to embody key relationships between objects. Views were defined for this project in keeping with the identified objective of exploring a new interface style using visually rich, highly realistic metaphors. As such, based on the prominence of the CD and relative unimportance of a player in our subject model, we decided to base our views on the real-world metaphor of a CD jewel case. The abstract modeling of views fully supported this approach, but could just as easily have supported other view paradigms, such as the windows, icons, and menus of a more conventional approach.

We ended up defining two views of the CD, to correspond to a closed and opened CD jewel case. Each of these views contained nested views of various related objects, such as the playlist, the tracks in the playlist, the CD artwork, and so forth. We even included a view of a book inside the view of the opened CD case; this extended our object model to include a book, which in turn contained information about each of the other objects in the model.

Despite the interest in designing a new interface style using real-world metaphors, it should be pointed out that the views defined in the model were defined for the purpose of supporting users' tasks. Rather than fitting required tasks into a preconceived view structure, we conceived the view structure as a means for accommodating all required tasks in an effective manner. Task analysis had identified the required tasks, but with approximately 40 tasks to be supported, it was necessary to arrange them in an appropriate manner. We decided on a model of progressive disclosure, which reveals simple functions in the base view and progressively more functions as the user progresses further within the interface. The metaphor of a case that opens to reveal additional information and functions and a book for even more information and functions fits the model of progressive disclosure perfectly.

Having identified views, we were then able to allocate tasks to those views according to the priority or importance of the tasks. This was facilitated by using a list, as shown in Figure A.6, in which all user actions are enumerated and dispositions of those tasks are documented across each view.

As tasks were allocated to views, those views were further defined in terms of the need for mechanisms to support each of the user actions within a given view. As indicated in Figure A.6, each action listed under each of the views is described in terms of a user interface control or mechanism for performing the action. This helps us further define the abstract model, as shown in Figure A.7. As we have already seen, views are incorporated in the object model as objects themselves. Likewise, the view objects are modeled further, to include all components of the view. This helps ensure the completeness of the design, and also forms clear documentation of requirements for interaction techniques and visual design.

User Action	Description	Base	Full	Book
Play	Play playlist from current position according to play settings	Play/Pause Control	Play/Pause Control	X
Pause	Pause	Play/Pause Control	Play/Pause Control	X
Stop	Stop playing, set current position to beginning of 1st track in playlist	Stop Control	Stop Control	X
Track forward	Go to next track in playlist unless at last track. If Continuous Play is On, then loop around	Fwd Control (Click)	Fwd Control (Click)	X
Position forward	Advance position within the current track until the end.	Fwd Control (Press)	Fwd Control (Press)	X
Track backward	If current position <10 seconds into track, go to previous track in playlist unless at first track in playlist. If >10 seconds, go to beginning of current track. If then loop around.	Bkwd Control (Click)	Bkwd Control (Click)	X
Position backward	Rewind position within the current track until the beginning	Bkwd Control (Press)	Bkwd Control (Press)	X
Eject	Open CD drive to eject CD	Eject Control	Eject Control	X
Switch Views	Change view to specified view	Switch View Control	Switch View Control	X
Put Away	Shut down ("Close") RealCD object (& book)	Put Away Control	Put Away Control	X
Put AwayBook	Close RealCD book and put back in CD case	X	X	"Put away book" control
Minimize	Minimize RealCD window to task bar (note task bar limitations for Java)	X	X	X
Set Random. On/Off	Randomizes Playlist / Resets Playlist	???	???	X
Set Continuous On/Off	Loop Play back / Don't Loop	???	???	X
Set Current Track	Sets current track directly to a specific track in playlist	X	set current track indicator to specific	X
Set Track On/Off	Sets Track On/Off in the playlist	X	Play/Don't Play Control	X
Reposition Track	Repositions Tracks within the playlist	X	Drag/Drop of Track Field Within Playlist Field	X
Adjust audio out	Launches Win95 Volume control	???	???	X
Move CD	Moves RealCD window (and Book window when appropriate)	Drag CD	Drag CD	
Edit CD title	Edit-in-place text, updates all CD title labels	X	Edit-in-place label	X
Edit Track title	Edit-in-place text, updates all title labels for that track	X	Edit-in-place label	X
Move Book	Moves Book window	X	X	Drag book
Open Book	Opens cover of book in place	X	X	Open Cover Control
Close Book	Closes book in place	X	X	Close Cover Control
Turn page	Turns to next page in sequence away from the spine	X	X	Page Turning Control
Add tracks to playlist	Ejects disc, prompts for next disc, appends tracks to current playlist	X	Add tracks control	
Reset Playlist Order	Resets Playlist order to original (that on CD itself)	X	X	Reset Order Control on Playlist page
Select CD Clip Art	Assign artwork to CD Cover, CD Spine, Book Cover, ...	X	X	CD Clip Art Selector
Customize CD Art	Note: done through Windows...replacing content of CD folder in Library	X	X	X

FIGURE A.6 *A more detailed list of user actions, with tasks allocated across views.*

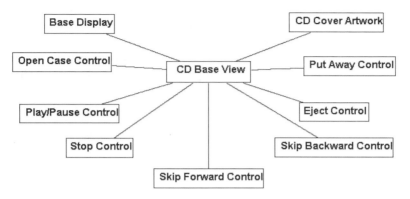

FIGURE A.7   *An object relationship diagram for a view of the CD object (note how the individual elements of this view clearly establish and document requirements for visual design).*

A.3.3 Interaction Design

Interaction design is also driven by users' requirements. A complete design must specify interactions for performing each task. Interactions may also be required for multiple input techniques, such as with a keyboard, mouse, and voice. The table excerpt shown in Figure A.8 facilitated this part of the design and helped ensure design completeness. The list itemizes the user actions already defined, and includes columns for each interaction technique. Such a table can serve as a checklist for the designer to follow to ensure completeness of the design.

User Action	Pointer	Keyboard
		Note: below plus cursor navigation
Play	Click Play/Pause Control	Enter
Pause	Click Play/Pause Control	Shift + Enter
Stop	Click Stop Control	Esc
Track forward	Click Fwd Control	Right Arrow Click
Position forward	Press Fwd Control	Right Arrow Press
Track backward	Click Bkwd Control	Left Arrow Click
Position backward	Press Bkwd Control	Left Arrow Press
Eject	Click Eject Control	
Switch Views	Click Switch View Control	Pg Dn / Pg Up
Put Away (Power off)	Click Put Away Control	Shift + End
Put Away Book	Drag/Drop, plu	Shift + End

FIGURE A.8   *A list itemizing all user actions and the interactions for supporting those tasks for both mouse and keyboard input.*

A.3.4 Visual Design

Visual design was involved throughout the RealCD project, and early visualizations of the object model helped to determine the metaphor and view structure of the design. Thus, visual design helped define the finished model, and the model helped to specify clear requirements for the final visuals.

A visual designer can provide valuable input, even early in the design process, doing sketches to visualize the model or further define it. (See Figure A.9.)

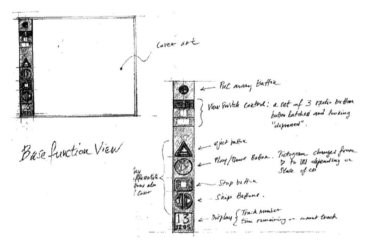

FIGURE A.9 *A visual designer's sketches of the RealCD interface.*

The enumerated elements in the object model serve as a checklist for visual elements. As shown in Figure A.10, each element is matched with the visual rendering of its primary state.

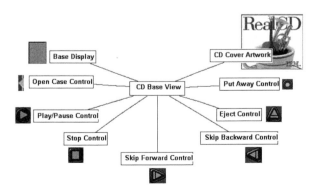

FIGURE A.10 *Elements matched with a visual rendering of their primary states.*

Each element or control is further defined in the model by its state diagram. Figure A.11 provides another checklist for visual design, where a unique visual rendering is usually needed for each state of the control.

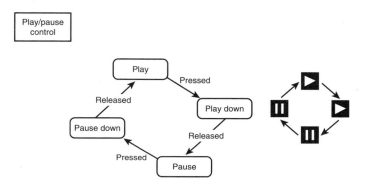

FIGURE A.11   *A visual rendering for each state of the control.*

At several times during the design process, prototypes were produced and tested in a variety of ways. Early pencil sketches were used for design walkthroughs, which helped to focus on the metaphor and narrow in on a particular visual style. Early walkthroughs also helped to reveal additional requirements, which were added to the task requirements and later factored into the design. To address minor design issues, lightweight interactive prototypes were rapidly built and informally tested among members of the team. Some prototypes were also distributed, along with a questionnaire, via Lotus Notes, to a broader internal community for evaluation. With each prototype and test, helpful improvements were factored into the design.

A.3.5 Implementation

With the design thus largely defined, implementation in Java was begun. This was the development team's first experience with the Java language and framework, but the implementation proceeded quickly. The final details of both design and implementation were worked out in parallel, with iteration through the characteristics of Java, which influenced the design to some extent. Certain behaviors and visual effects called for by the design were not supported by the early version of Java being used. For example, to indicate that the CD case could be resized by users, the original design called for the pointer to be displayed as directional arrows over the edges of the CD case. However, the version of Java being used could not support the pointer change as desired. The design was modified for the edges of the case to be highlighted when the pointer passes over them. This was documented in the state diagram of the CD case object, where an additional visual state was added. The updated object model, with the additional visual state for the CD case, served as a new requirement for visual design. Thus the requirements were clear for both visual design and implementation.

A.3.6 Iteration

The preceding example of modifying the design for Java is typical of the kind of iteration that might occur during the course of a software development project. The value provided by OVID in this case is that the abstract modeling of design decisions and modifications is used to clearly document these modifications. The abstract models can then clearly document change requirements for visual design and implementation.

In addition to the iteration that occurs constantly as design is done, iteration is also an important part of the process of prototyping and testing designs. Through prototyping and testing, user feedback is collected, which can help ensure that the final product will satisfy users.

For the RealCD project, a widespread beta test was conducted when the implementation reached an appropriate level of completion. This beta test was conducted by posting RealCD to the IBM Human–Computer Interaction intranet web site. Using an online questionnaire for user feedback, the beta test was inexpensive and easy to do. The feedback provided helped us to further iterate the design and implementation, which was very helpful in our efforts to finalize the project. To address some problems uncovered through the beta test, we did one more iteration of the design and implementation, and then announced RealCD on the World Wide Web in March 1997. (See Figures A.12 and A.13.)

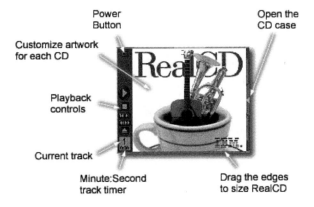

FIGURE A.12 *The final product.*

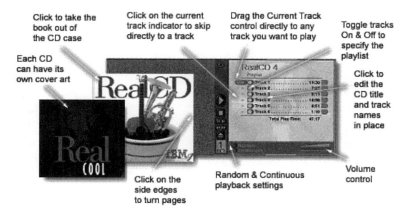

Click to take the
book out of
the CD case

Click on the current
track indicator to skip
directly to a track

Drag the Current Track
control directly to any
track you want to play

Toggle tracks
On & Off to
specify the
playlist

Each CD
can have its
own cover art

Click to
edit the
CD title
and track
names
in place

Click on the
side edges
to turn pages

Random & Continuous
playback settings

Volume
control

FIGURE A.13   *The implemented view is composed of all the individual visual elements.*

However, iteration did not end when RealCD was announced on the Web. In fact, the Web provided an excellent way to collect more user feedback. By including an online survey on the RealCD Web site, we collected numerous comments and survey responses. Based on that feedback, one more iteration was done, and an updated version was put on the Web.

APPENDIX B

Exercises

This appendix contains exercises that you can use to practice OVID. The materials are provided as a sequence of exercises. Each exercise builds on the previous ones and contains a possible solution for the previous stage. Try to work on how you would solve each stage before you read the next one.

Exercises like these can only provide a small insight into the experience of OVID. The largest missing elements are the direct contact with users and the opportunity to iterate on a solution. Practice here then try OVID on a real project.

B.1 Exercise 1: Find the First Objects
B.1.1 Materials

The scene of these exercises is a car service station. You have been called in to design a computer system to control the scheduling of the service operations. In each of the following sections you'll use different components of OVID to design a user-friendly, object-oriented system.

Booking a Service

Each vehicle is booked in for a particular service. The contact number for the owner/customer must be recorded in the diary, along with all other details. Special instructions from a customer must also be noted.

In some cases only certain operatives can carry out some types of service. Certain items of specialized equipment are needed in some cases. Each kind of service has an estimated duration. A service bay will be occupied for the duration of the service. In many cases a list of required parts will be available for a service; some of these may need to be ordered.

Arriving with the Vehicle

The customer will normally bring his or her vehicle to the service station at the beginning of the service. The customer may require help with transport.

A worksheet is used to inform the operatives which actions are to be performed. Vehicle keys are tagged, so that they can be identified and associated with a worksheet. The tag number and any last-minute instructions from the customer are recorded. Worksheets and tagged keys are placed in a set of trays, forming a queue of work.

Special Actions During Service

If it is anticipated that the estimated repair cost will be exceeded, then the customer must give permission for work to proceed.

Sometimes a service has to be suspended while unanticipated parts are ordered. Depending on the state of the vehicle when the service is suspended, it may be possible to free up a service bay while parts are awaited.

Sometimes a procedure may take longer than expected. The customer must be informed and special arrangements made.

Completing a Service

Comments from the operative should be recorded so that these can be given to the customer when he or she collects the vehicle. When work has finished, the customer should be informed and collection arranged. In the case of a regular maintenance service, the vehicle is recorded so that a reminder can be sent to the owner when the next service is due.

A bill must be prepared for the customer so that it is ready when he or she collects the vehicle. For service related to warranty, the vehicle manufacturer will pay the bill or some part of it.

B.1.2 Activity

As the first stage of the analysis, you must find the three to five most important objects to be implemented.

Study the information from a task analysis and fill in the table provided. Pick out the essential objects from the table and draw a diagram of these that shows the most significant relationships.

Hints for Finding Objects

- Underline each noun in the task analysis, and double-underline the names of real, physical objects.

- Write a one-sentence description of each object. Each sentence should have only one clause: no ifs, ands, or buts. If you cannot write such a sentence for any object, then you have probably bundled several objects into one. Split that object until the descriptions fit the rules.

- Record the number of times a particular object occurs in each task and weight these counts according to the frequency of the task. Work on those objects with a higher score first.

- Exclude objects that are in the task descriptions only because of the present method of performing the task (for example, an object that is a form used today). These will clutter analysis, and if they are really needed, you will prove it during task design.

- Sort the objects into the categories shown in Figure B.1, writing them in the appropriate columns. Use the space provided in Figure B.2 to draw an initial class diagram. At this stage you should only place the most important objects—probably three to five objects—in the diagram. Draw the most important relationships between the objects. You should find most of these objects in the leftmost column of Figure B.1.

Concrete Objects	People (Object)	Forms	People (Subjects)	Abstract

FIGURE B.1 *Objects found.*

FIGURE B.2 *Space for an initial class diagram.*

B.2 Exercise 2: More Analysis

In this section you'll add the remaining objects to the class diagram. First take the objects from the leftmost column in Figure B.1. Working from left to right in this fashion will help you to add the most important objects first.

B.2.1 Materials

Figure B.3 shows one way you might complete the table in Figure B.1. As you continue with these exercises, you may either use these objects or the ones you found earlier. Figure B.4 shows a possible version of a class diagram. Again, you can build on this diagram or the one you drew in Figure B.2.

Concrete Objects	People (Object)	Forms	People (Subjects)	Abstract
Vehicle Specialized equipment	**Owner/ Customer** Operative	Diary Worksheet Bill		Contact number Other details?
Service Bay Required part(s)/ unanticipated part(s)				Special instructions Type of service
Service Station Tagged keys Tray/queue of work				Estimated duration Help with transport
				Estimated repair cost
				Permission
				Comments (operative)
				Reminder

FIGURE B.3   *A possible way to sort the objects found.*

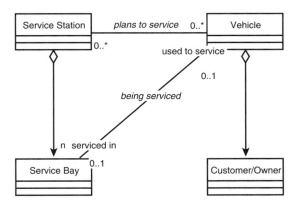

FIGURE B.4 *A possible class diagram for the objects found.*

B.2.2 Activity

Use Figure B.5 to continue to model the service station application by incorporating the objects from the table shown in Figure B. 3 into the designer's model diagram shown in Figure B.4.

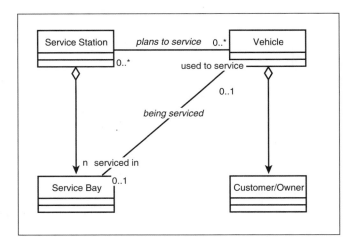

FIGURE B.5 *A worksheet for completing the service station application diagram.*

B.3 Exercise 3: Adding a View

Users can only work with objects when a view is provided. In this section you must add a view to the diagram that allows the operative to select the next vehicle for service.

B.3.1 Materials

Figure B.6 shows the class diagram for the application before the view is added.

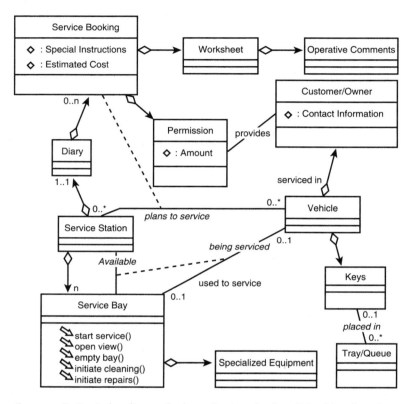

FIGURE B.6   *A class diagram for the application, showing all the objects from the scenario.*

B.3.2 Activity

Add a view to the user model diagram that allows an operative to select the next vehicle he or she must work on. Figure B.7 is a reduced form of the diagram in figure B.6 that allows you to add the required view.

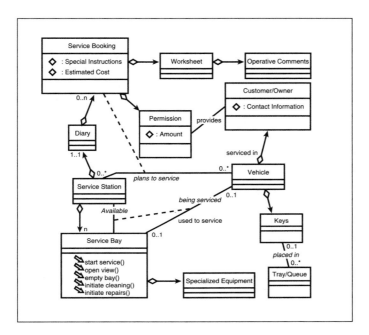

FIGURE B.7 *A worksheet for adding a view to the service station class diagram.*

B.4 Exercise 4: Document a Task

In this exercise, you'll use an interaction diagram to show how the operative selects the next vehicle for service.

B.4.1 Materials

Figure B.8 shows the class diagram for the application, including a Next vehicle view. Figure B.9 provides a blank interaction diagram for you to fill in.

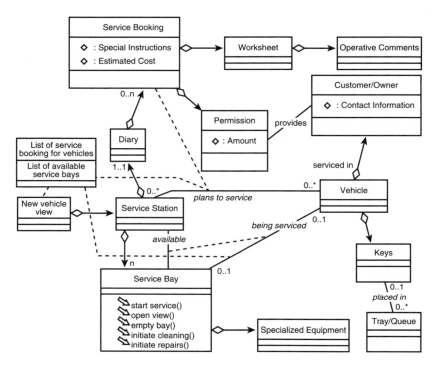

FIGURE B.8   *The class diagram with a Next vehicle view added.*

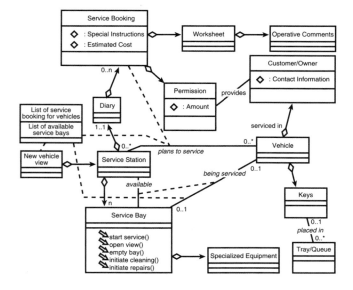

FIGURE B.9   *A worksheet for creating the interaction diagram for selecting the next vehicle.*

B.4.2 Activity

Based on the previous objects and views, use Figure B.10 to draw the task flow of the operative selecting the next vehicle to work on and allocating it to the service bay.

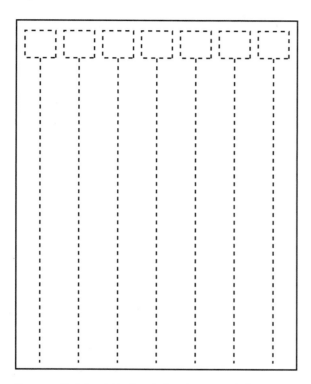

FIGURE B.10   *A blank task flow diagram, which you use to select the next vehicle.*

B.5 Exercise 5: State Diagram to Complete the Model

You will need to consider the state model for each object in the application. In this exercise you will create the model for the service bay.

B.5.1 Materials

Notice that we have added another view, the Service Bay view, which is used by the Next Vehicle view to show the details of each bay. This is typical of the way detail is added to the diagram as analysis proceeds. Figure B.11 is an interaction diagram for selecting the next vehicle for service. Figure B.12 is an interaction diagram for completing a service. You might create several scenarios where actions are done in a different order. Here the next vehicle is selected first by the operative; the view responds by altering the highlighting.

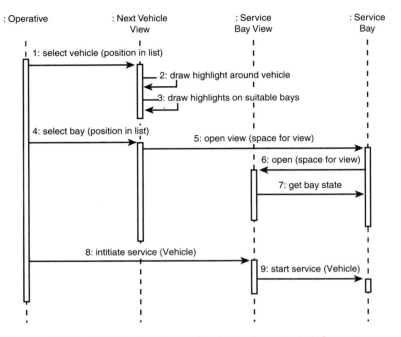

FIGURE B.11 *An interaction diagram for selecting the next vehicle for service.*

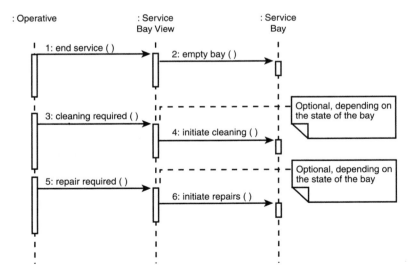

FIGURE B.12 *An interaction diagram for completing a service.*

B.5.2 Activity

Use Figures B.13 and B.14 to draw the state diagram and state table for the service bay.

Two of the scenarios involving the service bay were shown previously. Examine all of the prior material to see if there are any other scenarios.

Design Hints for Interactions

- Circle all the verbs in the task analysis. Check them against the transitions for an object. Each verb that does not have a corresponding transition should be carefully considered. There should be a reasonable explanation for any absence.

- On occasion, "islands" of states may be observed in the Harel (or state) diagram. These are clusters of states that have no transitions connecting them to other states. This pattern is an indication that two objects have been merged. In such cases a new object should be added and named to hold the states from one of the islands. The new object becomes a property of the object in which it was found.

- Whenever there is a *can't happen* condition for a state, all transitions to that state must disable any controls that could cause that event.

FIGURE B.13   *A blank state diagram. Fill it in for a service bay.*

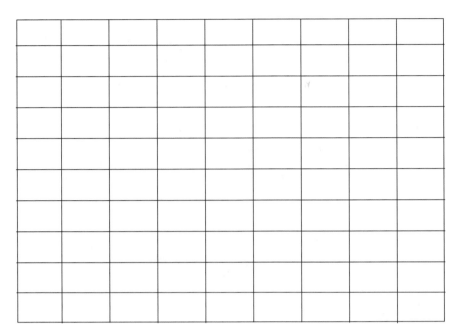

FIGURE B.14   *A blank state table. Fill it in for a service bay.*

B.5.3 Answers to Exercise 5

Figures B.15 and B.16 show the answers to Exercise B.5. Compare them against what you drew in Figures B.13 and B.14.

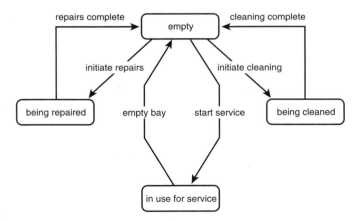

FIGURE B.15   *An initial state diagram of a service bay.*

	Empty	Being Cleaned	Being Repaired	In Use for Service
Empty Bay	Don't care.	Don't care.	Don't care.	Send *make ready* to open views. Go to Empty.
Start Service	Go to *In Use for Service*.	Not allowed.	Not allowed.	Not allowed.
Initiate Repairs	Send *make not ready* to open views. Go to *Being Repaired*.	? See 1.	Not allowed.	? See 2.
Repairs Complete	Should not happen.	Should not happen.	Send *make ready* to open views. Go to *Empty*.	Should not happen.
Initiate Cleaning	Send *make not ready* to open views. Go to *Being Cleaned*.	Not allowed.	? See 1.	? See 2.
Cleaning Complete	Should not happen.	Send *make ready* to open views. Go to *Empty*.	Should not happen.	Should not happen.

FIGURE B.16 *The state table for a service bay.*

In each of the four cells marked with ? there is a difficult design decision to be made. Here's an example:

1. Should the operative be allowed to initiate repairs while the bay is being cleaned or initiate cleaning while the bay is being repaired? The answer is probably yes, and this can be confirmed by reading the scenario for completing a service where both are optional actions. If this decision is accepted, then the service bay object would have to be remodeled. A possible new model is shown later in this appendix.

2. In the case of initiating repair or cleaning while the bay is in use, this could be considered a shortcut for going to empty and then on to being cleaned or repaired. The implementation of these changes would depend upon how the first question was answered.

The State Diagram of the Service Bay View

Figure B. 17 shows the communication between the object and the open views of that object. Notice that when the state of the service bay changes so that it cannot accept certain transitions, it signals this change to the view. The corresponding state diagram for the view is shown in Figure B.18.

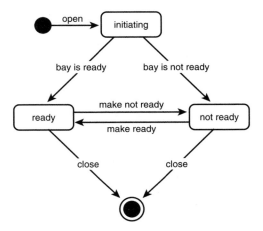

FIGURE B.17 *A state diagram for a service bay with all cells considered and filled with appropriate answers.*

	Closed[1]	Initiating[2]	Ready	Not Ready
Open	Go to *Initiating*.	Don't care.	Don't care.	Don't care.
Bay Is Ready	Don't care.	Go to *Ready*.	Can't happen.	Can't happen.
Bay Is Not Ready	Don't care.	Go to *Not Ready*.	Can't happen.	Can't happen.
Close	Don't care.	Don't care.	Close view.	Close view.
Make Ready[3]	Don't care.	Ensure that we go to the *Ready* state—some timing problem internally.	Don't care.	Set view to enable service initiation. Go to *Ready*.
Make Not Ready[4]	Don't care.	Ensure that we go to the *Not Ready* state—some timing problem internally.	Set view to disable service initiation. Go to *Not Ready*.	Don't care.

1 For the purpose of this figure, the start and end states are considered to be the same and are titled *Closed*.

2 This is a transient internal state during which the view is initializing itself. On entry to the state, the state of the service bay is examined and then one of the two exit transitions is taken.

3 This signal would come from the service bay to indicate that it had changed state.

4 This signal would come from the service bay to indicate that it had changed state.

FIGURE B.18 *A revised state diagram for a service bay.*

An Alternative Model for the Service Bay

Here the service bay is simplified so that it has only three states: empty, not available, and in use for service. The not available state is a replacement for both being cleaned and being repaired.

The object diagram would look like as shown in Figure B.19.

FIGURE B.19   *A revised harel diagram for a service bay.*

The action objects are used to hold the information about each of the uncompleted actions (repair or cleaning).

B.6 Summary

In these exercises we have only been able to look at a few parts of a design for a service station application. We added just one view, and one task, and worked on the state model for only one of the objects. We chose the examples because they bring out some of the issues that you are likely to meet during design. You could use this exercise as a basis for further practice by adding all the other views, state models, and interaction diagrams for all the duties mentioned in the initial scenario. Going beyond these exercises, we suggest that you begin to use OVID for a small project of your own.

Glossary

action   In task analysis, the set of activities required, used, or believed to be necessary to achieve a goal.

affordance   A tangible aspect of an object that suggests and permits some sort of action.

analysis   The application of some rational technique for decomposing a complex whole into its elements.

architecture   A general plan or set of concepts or principles governing the construction of some type of system.

association object (in a class diagram)   An object used to record information about one instance of a *many-to-many* association. Here a reservation records details of the *plan-to-stay* relationship between hotel and guest:

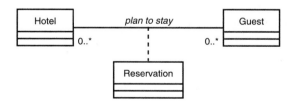

attribute (of an object in a class diagram)   An intrinsic part of an object's composition. Attributes can be shown inside the rectangle for an object (see object) or they can be shown using a *has a* relationship.

cardinality (in a class diagram)   The numbers at the point where the lines join the objects tell how many instances of that class of object can be involved in the relationship. Here we have said that any number of guests can plan to stay at a specific hotel and a guest can have any number of plans:

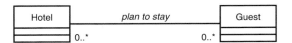

The cardinality of a relationship is shown using the following symbols:

Cardinality Notation	Meaning
0	None. This is not used much because it indicates a relationship that cannot happen.
1	Exactly one.
n	Some fixed number. Specific integer values may also be used as appropriate (e.g., 4, 12, etc.).
0..*	Zero or more.
1..*	One or more.
0..1	Zero or one.

CASE (computer-aided [or assisted] software design)   The use of computers to support software engineering processes.

class   A categorization or grouping of objects that share similar behaviors and characteristics.

class diagram   A diagram that shows the classes of objects that the user should be aware of and the relationships between them. This is an example of a class diagram showing some of the relationships between three objects: hotel, room, and guest. The lines between the rectangles show that hotel contains some rooms, a guest may *plan to stay* in a hotel, and a guest may stay in a room:

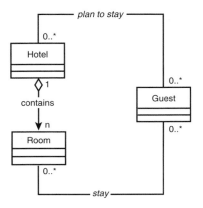

class hierarchy   A collection of object classes organized to indicate the other classes from which they have inherited various attributes.

composed view   A view of an object in which relationships of the parts contribute to the overall meaning. Composed views are provided primarily for data objects.

composite object   An object that contains other objects, usually of a different type (for example, a document object that contains not only text but graphics or image objects, which may each be separate objects).

container object   An object whose specific purpose is to hold other objects.

containment   The principle that objects hold other objects and can be held by other objects.

controls   User interface components that allow a user to interact with data.

design   The process of creating a plan or "blueprint" for building something, or the plan created by this process. In the development of computer applications or systems, design takes the output of analysis and specifies a concrete system that will satisfy the users' requirements.

designer's model   A representation of the way the designer wants the user to understand the system. The designer's model bridges the users' model to the programmer's model.

end state (in a class diagram)   A notation for a state on a state diagram that is the target (end point) of any events that destroy an object of that class. The dark circle in the following Harel diagram indicates an end state:

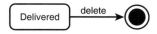

event (in an interaction diagram)   An arrow drawn between objects to indicate an action that one object performs on another (or itself). In this example, a reservation is sending the view event to a guest:

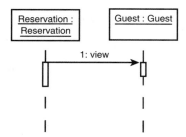

finite state machine   A system in which an object is always in one known state, and there is a fixed list of these states.

goal   In task analysis, the state of a system that a person wants to achieve.

GUI (graphical user interface)   A user interface based on bitmapped graphics as opposed to character display.

Harel diagram   *See* state diagram.

has a **(in a class diagram)**   An aggregation represented as a diamond on a line. Here the guest has a street address. The text on the line shows why the street address is the one used for billing. The name should be given from the perspective of the owning object, in this case the guest:

hierarchical task analysis   A method for collecting and documenting user tasks that creates graphical representations of high-level tasks broken into constituent tasks and actions.

implementor's model   *See* programmer's model.

inheritance   The principle that objects acquire attributes from other classes of objects.

instance   A particular object, as opposed to a class of objects (for example, the dog Spot is an instance of the class dog).

instantiation   The process of creating a new instance of a class.

interaction diagram   *See* sequence diagram.

metaphor   A word, phrase, or visual representation that denotes or depicts one object or idea, but suggests a likeness or analogy with another object.

model   The conceptual and operational understanding that a person has about something.

naming conventions (in a state diagram)   A consistent pattern for labeling items in a state diagram. Some changes in an object happen at the request of the user. Other changes happen as a result of some other part of the system. To avoid confusion over the source of an action, each user action may be identified. In OVID we recommend that you prefix all user events with the letter U and a colon, as in the following diagram:

U:clean

Occupied

object   A component of a user interface that a user can work with to perform a task.

object (in a class diagram)   A rectangle labeled with the name of the class. In this case, the object is a room, and it is shown with the attributes smoking and bed:

Room
: Smoking
: Bed

object (in an interaction diagram)   A column in which the name is written in two parts—instance:class—because there may be cases where several instances of the same class are involved in an interaction. In the following example, an instance of the class room is named free room:

Free room :
Room

object decomposition   The process of breaking an object into its component parts.

object hierarchy   A way of illustrating relationships among objects. Each object that appears in a level below another object is an example of the upper object.

object orientation   A style of user interface in which a user's attention is directed toward the objects the user works with to perform a task.

object–oriented analysis   An analysis in which the problem decomposition results in a set of objects and classes, the relationships between them, and the services they provide—or the process of doing such an analysis.

object–oriented programming   A system of organizing programming where the code is divided into modules called *objects*. The objects communicate with each other by passing messages.

object–oriented user interface   A type of user interface that implements the object-action paradigm.

object subclass   An object created from another object and from which the properties of the original object are inherited.

object superclass   The object from which subclass objects are created. The properties of the superclass object are inherited by the subclass object.

OVID (Object, View, and Interaction Design)   A methodology for design of user interfaces.

Paradigm   An example, a pattern, or a model.

programmer's model   A representation of a product or computer system from the perspective of the person who writes the code that makes the product or system work. Also called an *implementor's model*.

properties   The particular characteristics and attributes of an object.

prototype   A mock-up of a proposed system that allows inspection and testing to begin before the final product has been built. Rapid prototyping is the technique of building a prototype as quickly as possible to guide the early stages of analysis or design.

Rational Rose   A software modeling tool.

relationship (in a class diagram)   A line between two classes represents a relationship between those classes. In this example, the guest and hotel participate in a *plan to stay* relationship:

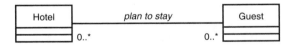

scenario   An outline of tasks and subtasks that describes how users will do their work.

sequence diagram   A diagram that shows a sequence of events and how they are passed from one object to another. Also called an *interaction diagram*. In the following diagram, a sequence of messages pass when a user checks in a guest to a room in a hotel:

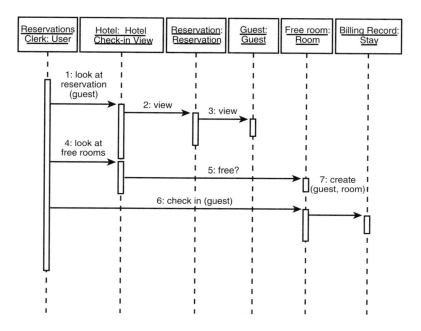

spiral life–cycle model   A software development process in which there is iteration between development phases.

start state (in a class diagram)   A special notation for a state on a state diagram that is the origin of any events that create an object of that class. In the following diagram, an object moves from its start state to an empty state when the create event occurs:

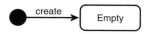

state (in a state diagram)   A rounded rectangle shows a state, and the name of the state is shown inside. In the following diagram, an object has a state named Free:

state diagram   A diagram that is used to show the states that an object can have. This sample shows the possible life cycle of a guest message:

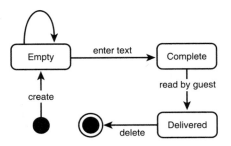

state table   A table that shows the same information as a state diagram. The table is constructed with one column for each state and one row for each possible event. Here is an example of a table for a simple check box:

	State	
Event	not checked	checked
press	transition to *checked*	transition to *not checked*
release	ignore	ignore

state transition (in a state diagram)   A change in one state cause by a change in an object. An arrow indicates the next state and text describes what happened. In the following example, an object changes from Free to Occupied because of a check in event:

state transition that returns to the same state (in a state diagram)   When there is no state change for an event, the arrow in a state diagram loops back to the state it came from. Here, whenever an occupied room is cleaned, it remains occupied:

subclass (in a class diagram) A notation that indicates that one class is a special version of another class. Here a penthouse suite and a honeymoon suite are special types of rooms:

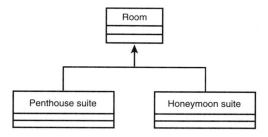

task A meaningful unit of work, composed of a series of steps that lead to some well-defined goal.

task analysis The process of investigating a problem by breaking down tasks that potential users of a system do or would do into sequences of actions and objects.

use case scenario An outline of tasks and subtasks that describes how users will do their work.

user interface The area where a user and an object come together to interact. As applied to computers, it is the ensemble of hardware and software that allows a user to interact with a computer.

users' conceptual model The concepts and expectations a person develops through experience.

***uses* or *depends on* (in a class diagram)** A dotted line with an arrow is a uses relationship or dependency between objects. Here the hotel view for check-in depends on or uses the guest details view:

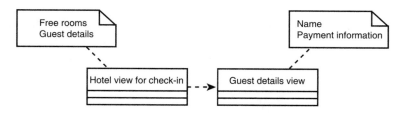

view The form in which an object is presented. For example, a window on the screen may show a view of an object, or a sound from a speaker may be a view of some music.

view (in a class diagram)   A notation for showing how a view is derived from the objects in a class diagram. In this sample diagram, the Hotel view for check-in belongs to the hotel, and it shows free rooms and guest details:

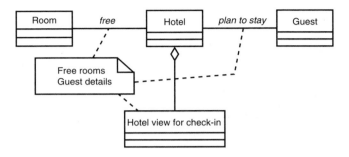

waterfall life-cycle model   A sequential process of software development with little or no overlap or iteration between and among phases.

Bibliography

Apple Computer Inc. 1992. *Macintosh Human Interface Guidelines*. Reading, MA: Addison-Wesley.

Berry, R. 1992. The designer's model of the CUA workplace. *IBM Systems Journal*, vol. 31, no. 3.

Berry, R., and C. Reeves. 1992. The evolution of the Common User Access workplace model. *IBM Systems Journal*, vol. 31, no. 3.

Boar, B. 1984. *Application Prototyping: A Requirements Definition Strategy for the 80s*. New York: John Wiley & Sons.

Boehm, B. 1981. *Software Engineering Economics*. Englewood Cliffs, NJ: Prentice Hall.

Boehm, B. 1988. A spiral model of software development and enhancement. *IEEE Computer*, May.

Booch, G. 1994. *Object-Oriented Analysis and Design*. Redwood City, CA: Benjamin/Cummings.

Brooks, F., Jr. 1986. No silver bullet. *Information Processing '86*. New York: Elsevier Science Publishers.

Casey, S. 1993. *Set Phasers on Stun: And Other True Tales of Design, Technology, and Human Error*. Santa Barbara, CA: Aegean Publishing Co.

Catterall, B., B. Taylor, and M. Galer. 1991. The HUFIT planning, analysis, and specification toolset: Human factors and a normal part of the IT product design processing. In *Taking Software Seriously*, ed. J. Karat. London: Academic Press.

Collins, D. 1995. *Designing Object-Oriented User Interfaces*. Redwood City, CA:
Benjamin/Cummings.

Ericsson, K., and H. Simon. 1985. *Protocol Analysis: Verbal Reports as Data*.
Cambridge, MA: MIT Press.

Goldberg, A. 1990. Information models, views, and controllers. *Dr. Dobb's Journal*,
July, 54—60.

Hackos, J., and Redish, J. 1998. *User and Task Analysis for Interface Design*. New York:
John Wiley & Sons.

Hix, D., and H. R. Hartson. 1993. *Developing User Interfaces: Ensuring Usability
through Product and Process*. New York: John Wiley & Sons.

IBM Corp. 1992. *Object-Oriented Interface Design: IBM Common User Access
Guidelines*. Carmel, IN: Que.

Isensee, S., and J. Rudd. 1996. *The Art of Rapid Prototyping*. Boston: International
Thomson Computer Press.

Jacobson, I. 1992. *Object-Oriented Software Engineering: A Use Case Driven Approach*.
Reading, MA: Addison-Wesley.

Landauer, T. 1995. *The Trouble with Computers*. Cambridge, MA: MIT Press.

Manes, S. 1996. One step forward, two steps back with I.B.M. The *New York Times
SCIENCE*, October 22.

Microsoft Corporation. 1995. *The Windows Interface Guidelines for Software Design*.
Redmond, WA: Microsoft Press.

Mossberg, W. 1996. Computer makers take note: Cut the glitz, keep it simple, *Wall
Street Journal*.

Nelson, G. 1983. Design theory. In *Design Since 1945*. Philadelphia: Philadelphia
Museum of Art.

Nielsen, J. 1993. *Usability Engineering*. Chestnut Hill, MA: AP Professional.

Nielsen, J., and R. Mack. 1994. *Usability Inspection Methods*. New York: John Wiley
& Sons.

Nielsen, J., and R. Molich. 1990. Heuristic evaluation of user interfaces. In
Proceedings of CHI Conference on Human Factors in Computing Systems. New York:
ACM, 249—256.

Open Software Foundation. 1993. *OSF/Motif Style Guide*. Englewood Cliffs, NJ:
Prentice Hall.

Preece, J., Y. Rogers, H. Sharp, D. Benyon, S. Holland, and T. Carey. 1994. *Human–Computer Interaction*. Reading, MA: Addison-Wesley.

Redmond-Pyle, D., and A. Moore. 1995. *Graphical User Interface Design and Evaluation*. London: Prentice Hall.

Rubin, K., and A. Goldberg. 1992. Object behavior analysis. *Communications of the ACM*, September.

Rumbaugh, J. 1991. *Object-Oriented Modeling and Design*. Englewood Cliffs, NJ: Prentice Hall.

Sager, I., R. Hof, and P. Judge. 1996. The race is on to simplify. *Business Week Special Report*, June 24.

Schneiderman, B. 1998. *Designing the User Interface: Strategies for Effective Human–Computer Interaction,* Third Edition. Reading, MA: Addison-Wesley.

Shepard, A. 1989. Analysis and training in information tasks. In *Task Analysis for Human–Computer Interaction*, ed. D. Diaper. Chichester: Ellis Horwood.

Snyder, K. 1991. *A Guide to Software Usability*. IBM Corp.

Taylor, D. 1990. *Object-Oriented Technology: A Manager's Guide*. Reading, MA: Addison-Wesley.

Weinschenk, S., P. Jamar, and S. Yeo. 1997. *GUI Design Essentials*. New York: John Wiley & Sons.

Whiteside, J., J. Bennett, and K. Holtzblatt. 1988. Usability engineering: Our experience and evolution. In *Handbook of Human–Computer Interaction*, ed. M. Helander. Amsterdam: North-Holland.

Wirfs-Brock, R., B. Wilkerson, and L. Wiener. 1990. *Designing Object-Oriented Software*. Englewood Cliffs, NJ: Prentice Hall.

Wood, L. (ed.). 1998. *User Interface Design: Bridging the Gap from User Requirements to Design*. Boca Raton, FL: CRC Press.

Yourdon, E. 1989. *Modern Structured Analysis*. Englewood Cliffs, NJ: Yourdon Press.

Index

A

abstractions
    properties (views), defining, 104–105
    prototypes, 110, 112

accomodating
    programmer's limitations, 33–34
    varying user proficiencies, 30–32

acquiring domain knowledge, 52–53

actions
    diagramming, state machines, 89–91
    end user, analyzing, 63–69

actors
    interrelationships, documenting, 74–80
    role in use-case analysis, 68–69
    see also objects

aesthetic aspects (objects), 36–37

analyzing
    dimensions, 39
    software development, requirements, 47–48
    usability, 63–64
        task scenarios, documentation, 65–69
        use case, 67–69

applications
    hotel, field evalutation, 119
    models, prototypes, 109–110, 112–116
    selecting for programming model environment, 93–98
    usability testing, 121
        data analysis, 126
        data collection, 125
        designing tasks, 123–124
        preparing materials, 124
        selecting participants, 122–123

architecture, UI (user interface), 39

V–Z